DULY NOTED

Extend Your Mind Through Connected Notes

by

JORGE ARANGO

foreword by Howard Rheingold

TWO WAVES
BOOKS

TWO WAVES BOOKS
NEW YORK, NY, USA

"In an age of information overload, *Duly Noted* is a perfectly pitched guide to the principles and practices of connected thinking and tending to your personal knowledge garden."

—Andy Polaine
Leadership Coach and co-author of *Service Design: From Insight to Implementation*

"An excellent resource for practicing a vital skill, *Duly Noted* clearly and succinctly presents our options for developing our ideas in today's increasingly digital age."

— Kourosh Dini, MD
Author of *Taking Smart Notes with DEVONthink*

"A clear, useful and informative guide to turning your untamed thoughts—the wilderness of your mind—into a beautiful, organized, well-maintained garden."

—Dave Gray
Author of *Liminal Thinking*, co-author of *Gamestorming*, founder of the School of the Possible

Duly Noted
Extend Your Mind Through Connected Notes
By Jorge Arango

Rosenfeld Media, LLC
125 Maiden Lane
New York, New York 10038
USA

On the Web: www.rosenfeldmedia.com
Please send errata to: errata@rosenfeldmedia.com

Publisher: Louis Rosenfeld
Managing Editor: Marta Justak
Interior Layout: Danielle Foster
Cover Design: Heads of State
Indexer: Marilyn Augst
Proofreader: Sue Boshers

ISBN: 1- 959029-04-5
ISBN 13: 978-1-959029-04-5
LCCN: 2023945898

Printed and bound in the United States of America

To my parents, Jorge and Lilines,
who taught me that the point of learning
isn't accumulating ideas but acting more wisely.

Contents at a Glance

Foreword

Humans have created sciences and civilizations because we learned to create and share tools for thinking and knowing. Note-taking, whether it is on scraps of paper, notebooks, or smartphones, is a tool for thinking and knowing that practically everybody uses. Knowing how to use it well is a learnable skill—and now note-taking apps can amplify your ability to create "knowledge gardens," similar to the way word processing amplifies your ability to write and the internet amplifies your ability to communicate. This book and the practices it articulates will supercharge your note-taking, sense-making, and personal knowledge acquisition.

Starting with speech, and then gaining more power with writing, alphabets, printing, personal computers, and the internet, our ability to think and know has co-evolved with our knowledge tools. These tools magnify the power of our mind, the way physical tools, such as wheels and levers, magnify the power of our muscles. The key to supercharging your personal thinking and knowing power lies in how you use the thinking tools we have co-evolved. That's where education comes in. But educational institutions change slowly, while technologies have been changing quickly. Schools teach reading and writing, but so far, no school teaches advanced note-taking, knowledge gardening, or the use of note-taking apps such as Obsidian. This book addresses that gap.

Using nontechnical language and examples from everybody's everyday life, *Duly Noted* illuminates the power of knowledgeable note-taking in remembering, learning, creating, and knowing. From daily to-do lists to elaborate frameworks for writing books or teaching courses, the skills you learn from this book can empower every aspect of your daily life. You don't have to go to a university or master an esoteric new practice—we all have a lifetime of experience in note-taking. The author of this book, Jorge Arango, has mastered the practices necessary to turn your note-taking habits into a power tool for your mind.

Much of today's personal computing grows out of the work of Douglas Engelbart at Stanford Research Institute in the 1960s. In addition to the mouse, point-and-click interface, hypertext, on-screen outlining, and video on computer screens, Engelbart laid out a framework for using computer-based tools that he called "H/LAMT"—"humans using language, artifacts, methodology, and training." While the power of the artifact part of personal computing has multiplied a millionfold and more since Engelbart's time, the methodology and training parts of the regimen he imagined have hardly advanced. This book is the kind of advance Engelbart envisioned—computers and smartphones are mind amplifiers for those who know how to use them. Note-taking is such an integral part of daily life for so many that it's a mystery why it took so many decades for a comprehensive guide to note-taking as a cyber-powered thinking and knowing to emerge.

Unlike computer programming, you don't need to learn a new and alien language to supercharge note-taking. With a simple app and a simple methodology, you can quickly multiply the power of your present note-taking practices. With this book, your notebook or your smartphone can truly become a powerful tool for thinking and knowing.

—Howard Rheingold
Author of *Tools for Thought*

Introduction

On March 9, 2022, a bright pink shopping bag mysteriously appeared outside the office of the Cambridge University library. Inside the bag was a package containing two notebooks and a note that read:

> Librarian
>
> Happy Easter
>
> X

"Happy" underestimated the package's effect. The University's Director of Library Services, Jessica Gardner, said:

> My sense of relief at the notebooks' safe return is profound and almost impossible to adequately express. Along with so many others all across the world, I was heartbroken to learn of their loss and my joy at their return is immense.

Why such strong emotions? The bag contained two of Charles Darwin's notebooks, which had gone missing twenty years earlier and triggered an international police hunt. Gardner elaborated:

> They may be tiny, just the size of postcards, but the notebooks' impact on the history of science, and their importance to our world-class collections here, cannot be overstated.[1]

Heavy stuff! And appropriate: Darwin produced the two notebooks in the mid-1830s while formulating his theory of natural selection. One of them includes his famous sketch of the tree of life.

---

1. www.cam.ac.uk/stories/TreeOfLife

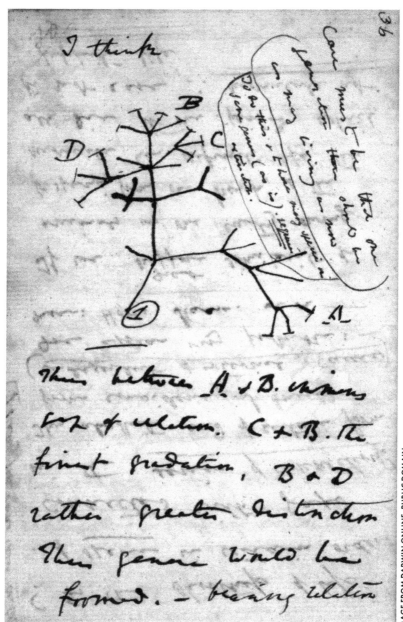

Charles Darwin's 1837 sketch of the evolutionary tree from his "B" notebook, one of two books that were returned to Cambridge University in 2022. Note the words "I think" at the top of the page—Darwin was making an abstract idea concrete.

So, these aren't just a couple of old books but important historical artifacts. Their value doesn't derive from their physical nature—after all, they're just stacks of bound paper—but from having served as crucibles for (and records of) world-changing ideas.

Like other great thinkers, Darwin used notes to augment his mind. These two notebooks were part of a series where he worked out scientific and personal issues. By 1840, he'd completed the series and moved on to a new system based on loose-leaf portfolios. At that point, he cut pages from his old notebooks and included them in the portfolios.[2]

Notes mattered to Darwin. And he wasn't alone: Leonardo da Vinci, Richard Feynman, and Virginia Woolf were among many brilliant thinkers and creators who worked out ideas using notes. Their notebooks have come to represent the potential of the human mind. Museums and collectors don't value them arbitrarily: important breakthroughs happened on their pages.

You, too, can expand your cognitive abilities using notes. Your innate memory—amazing as it is—has limits: you forget many things and misremember others. You already know that setting down thoughts helps you remember them later. But notes aren't just for remembering: they also let you work out complex ideas by making abstract notions concrete.

As you'll learn in this book, there's a key difference between *taking* notes and *making* notes: the former is about capturing ideas for recall, whereas the latter is about generating new ideas.[3] We'll cover both, but we'll pay particular attention to *note-making with computers*.

Thinking with Computers

Throughout history, most note-takers and note-makers used paper, which has many virtues as a medium. But in the 21st century, we have computers, which extend your mind in powerful new ways. And it's lucky they do, since computers also greatly increase the amount of information in the world. There's so much stuff today that new ways of thinking are called for.

The idea of using computers to augment thinking isn't new. In his 1985 book *Tools for Thought*, Howard Rheingold traced the field's history from Charles

---

2. http://darwin-online.org.uk/EditorialIntroductions/vanWyhe_notebooks.html
3. More on this distinction in Chapter 2.

Babbage and Ada Lovelace's 19th-century steampunk contraptions to Turing and von Neumann's vacuum tube calculating giants of the mid-20th-century to Licklider, Engelbart, and Kay's interactive computing and Nelson's hypertext visions in the second half of the century.[4]

Most of what you'll learn in this book originated from those earlier efforts. However, for a long time, implementations were either confined to research projects or, in some cases (such as Apple's pioneering *Hypercard* app), released too early to market. But that's changed in the past two decades.

Thanks to the internet, we're now producing and consuming more information than ever. More people are facing information overload. On the flip side, we've also become more comfortable using computers. The web, in particular, makes the crucial concept of hyperlinks familiar to billions of people.[5] And, of course, developing, acquiring, and learning software is easier and cheaper now than ever before.

So, you now have both the need and ability to think with computers on a scale and scope previously unimaginable. Tools like Delicious, Evernote, and Microsoft OneNote have been around since the turn of the century. But around 2020, new tools started to appear that provide powerful hypertext note-taking capabilities not seen outside research labs. Budding scenes emerged around personal knowledge management (PKM), tools for thinking, and "digital gardening."

Interest is wide enough that essays started to appear questioning the utility of digital note-taking systems. They sported titles such as *Is the Concept of Personal Knowledge Management Flawed?*; *Note-Taking Became a Full-time Job, so I Stopped*; *Personal Knowledge Management Is Exhausting*; and (classic!) *Personal Knowledge Management Is Bullshit*.

Objectors usually raise one or several of these points:

- Building and maintaining a note-taking system takes time and effort.
- You could be doing other things instead, including writing.
- Note-taking systems won't directly produce publishable artifacts.

---

4. H. Rheingold, *Tools for Thought: The History and Future of Mind-Expanding Technology* (Cambridge: MIT Press, 2000).
5. We'll look at hyperlinks in Chapter 3.

All are fair, but they misunderstand what notes are for and their role in the creative process. Digital note-taking systems won't think in your stead; while AI has progressed considerably in the last decade (more of this in Chapter 10), computers can't yet make sense of the stuff you capture.

What digital notes can do is help *you* think better. When you take notes, you explore the scope and boundaries of ideas. You think differently about things when considering how they might relate to other things. The point isn't to stash ideas for later or to have a machine think for you, but *to create a space that lets you think more effectively.*

A Garden for Thinking

What kind of space should you create? I like a metaphor with deep roots in the field: that of a garden.[6]

Building and tending a garden takes time and effort. Some gardens are small, personal projects that provide more satisfaction than nourishment. But with serious commitment, it's possible to build a garden that nourishes *and* delights. Unlike "products" like books or YouTube videos, gardens aren't meant to be *finished*: the point is to keep them going.

Which is to say, gardening provides value beyond mere utility. It's a contemplative practice that calls for patience, stewardship, and discipline—essential skills that are at risk of atrophying in our growth-hacked world. Maintaining a botanical garden or a knowledge garden is caring for something besides yourself, something that is alive and will keep you alive—literally and metaphorically.

In 1965, Ted Nelson noted that knowledge and creative work co-evolve with the technologies that enable them and speculated about the role computers might play. The purpose of these systems, he observed, shouldn't be to serve as static stores of knowledge but as dynamic media for thinking. As he put it:

> If a writer is really to be helped by an automated system, it
> ought to do more than retype and transpose: it should stand by

6. In *A Brief History & Ethos of the Digital Garden*, Maggie Appleton documented the use of gardening as a metaphor for digital note-taking in public. https://maggieappleton.com/garden-history
Appleton traces the earliest use to Mark Bernstein's 1998 essay "Hypertext Gardens." In an interview on my podcast, Bernstein noted an earlier use by Cathy Marshall at Xerox PARC. https://theinformed.life/2022/10/23/episode-99-mark-bernstein/

him during the early periods of muddled confusion, when his ideas are scraps, fragments, phrases, and contradictory overall designs. And it must help him through to the final draft with every feasible mechanical aid—making the fragments easy to find, and making easier the tentative sequencing and juxtaposing and comparing.[7]

Historian and Pulitzer Prize–winning author David McCullough said, "Writing is thinking. To write well is to think clearly. That's why it's so hard."[8] A personal knowledge garden won't write for you, but it will help you clarify relationships between fragmentary and often disparate thoughts, seeing you through "early periods of muddled confusion."

But again, it's hard work. And not everyone is either called or suited to do it.

So, who is this book for? It's for anyone who *thinks for a living*: knowledge workers, content creators, teachers, students, and more. Perhaps they're looking to master a subject for professional or academic reasons, or maybe they dream of writing a book or producing a YouTube channel. Whatever the case, they want to dive deeply into ideas and perhaps contribute some of their own.

The fact that you've picked up this book suggests you may see yourself in this camp. But if you don't, consider whether you'd benefit from a more mindful relationship with information. There's more of it every day, and without the means to manage it, you can quickly become overwhelmed.

Moreover, advancing in your career requires continually learning new things. Today, many of us work in areas that rely on acquiring, managing, and deploying knowledge. Whether you're a designer, computer programmer, doctor, teacher, etc., your effectiveness depends on your ability to find, assimilate, and produce information.

7. T. H. Nelson, "Complex Information Processing: A File Structure for the Complex, the Changing and the Indeterminate," *ACM '65: Proceedings of the 1965 20th National Conference*, August 1965, 84–100. Nelson's gendered language is an artifact of its time; obviously these ideas apply to everybody.
8. www.neh.gov/about/awards/jefferson-lecture/david-mccullough-biography

And it needn't be complicated. Although the underlying technologies are very sophisticated, thinking with digital notes boils down to three simple rules:

1. Make short notes.
2. Connect your notes.
3. Nurture your notes.

This book shows you how to do it.

What's in the Book?

The material is divided into ten chapters:

- Chapter 1, "Notes Are for Thinking," examines notes themselves: what they are, what they're good for, and what makes them different from other things you make.

- Chapter 2, "Make Short Notes," covers note-taking first principles, emphasizing several crucial distinctions you must know to take better notes.

- Chapter 3, "Connect Your Notes," shows you how to connect notes to create networks of ideas.

- Chapter 4, "Plan for a Knowledge Garden," lays out a plan for building an effective note-taking system: your personal knowledge garden.

- Chapter 5, "Don't Let Ideas Get Away," shows you how to capture ideas, so you don't lose them.

- Chapter 6, "Put Everything in Its Right Place," shows you how to organize your notes to let you find and make sense of them later.

- Chapter 7, "Spark Insights," explains how connected notes can lead you to discover new ideas and spark insights.

- Chapter 8, "Share Your Thinking," explains how and why to share what you learn—and also learn by sharing.

- Chapter 9, "Tend the Garden," covers the weeding and care of your knowledge garden.

- Chapter 10, "Think with Other Minds," shows you how to collaborate with other minds—including artificial ones.

Each chapter includes sidebars that aim to bring the material to life and make it more actionable. Each of these sections is labeled according to the following taxonomy:

- **Notable Note-Taker** sections showcase examples of how individuals use notes to augment their thinking.
- **Side Notes** offer advice and tips to spur you on your journey toward better thinking through note-taking.
- **Working Notes** include how-to exercises that will help you get started taking connected notes.

In the latter, you'll work through examples using a specific digital note-taking tool: Obsidian. I've chosen this app for various reasons:

- It's powerful yet easy to understand.
- It's available on macOS, Windows, Linux, and mobile devices.
- It has a thriving community of developers and users.
- It allows you to retain direct control of your data, so you can easily move your notes elsewhere.
- Although it's proprietary software, it's currently free for personal use.[9]

You don't have to use Obsidian to take advantage of the ideas in this book. Other applications provide most of the capabilities we'll discuss. And this is a fast-moving field: by the time you read this, several other interesting tools will likely have come to market. So, feel free to use a different tool if you prefer.[10]

If you're new to these ideas, *Duly Noted* will help you use information to generate knowledge more skillfully and productively. And if you're already building and using a digital note-taking system, you'll learn to use it more effectively. Whichever the case, I hope you have fun. Stewarding a personal knowledge garden has enriched and deepened my life. It can do so for you as well.

---

9. Some advanced Obsidian features, or using the tool for business purposes, require upgrading to a paid plan.
10. For a list of criteria for selecting a digital note-taking tool, see Chapter 9.

1

Notes Are for Thinking

When I was a boy, the beginning of school was one of my favorite times of the year. One day always stood out: when my mom took me to buy stationery. I loved getting new pens, pencils, and notebooks. A fresh notebook held the promise of clarity, order, and better grades. I mostly used Mead Trapper Keepers, a popular brand of loose-leaf binders. They represent how I managed notes as a kid: I'd write down what I heard during class and stash pages in that subject's section, in chronological order. While studying, I'd revisit those notes. Occasionally, I'd discard old ones to make room.

By the end of the school year, I had a binder full of transcripts. They'd served their purpose, so I could toss them. Next year would bring new teachers, new classes, and new notebooks. I seldom revisited old notes. This basic approach was the start of my note-taking life. I've since learned that notes can be more than a means for capture and recall: they're also a medium for thinking.

What Are Notes For?

My Mac's dictionary defines a note as "a brief record of facts, topics, or thoughts, written down as an aid to memory." But as with other common words, "note" has more than one meaning. We also speak of some financial instruments as notes. And, of course, notes are also the stuff of musical melodies. But in this book, we mean the first usage: brief written records that aid our minds.

Not everything you write down is a note. For one thing, as the definition says, notes tend to be short. Think sticky notes, not essays. Intent also matters: you make notes primarily to aid your thinking. Sometimes you write notes for others, but most often you do so for yourself. Some notes you "dash off," while others you ponder. Most aren't meant for publication; I've made many notes while writing this book, but writing the book's text is different from note-taking. All notes augment your mind in different ways.

Remembering

Remembering might be the most common reason to take notes: you hear or see something you want to recall later. This is why, when you call a company's help desk, the agent suggests you have a pen and paper at hand. It's good advice: such calls yield case numbers, dates, and other details that you'll forget quickly if you don't write them down.

Transcribing

A common reason for taking notes is to recall what you heard during a lecture or video. For example, when attending a presentation, you may type into your laptop or scribble in your notebook. Doing so has a dual benefit: it helps you pay attention and produces a text that reminds you of what the speaker said.

Recording

Some professions, such as research scientists and medical doctors, benefit from keeping records of their work. This is a kind of remembering, but a bit more formal. It's worth examining separately since such notes also provide legally admissible evidence when outcomes are contested. People in professions that require it take great care with their notes.

Learning

Sometimes you write things down not because you're trying to remember a particular detail but because you're trying to learn about a subject. Learning entails more than just remembering facts. For one thing, you must connect ideas at different levels of abstraction. For another, learning often happens in sessions spread over several days, weeks, or months, as in a class. Much of the note-taking discussed in this book focuses on learning.

Researching

When researching a subject, you want to recall the salient facts. And if you're interviewing someone, you want to keep track of the most important things they said. In either case, you're ultimately looking to synthesize what you learn so you can make better decisions. Notes aid the process.

Generating

Sometimes you take notes not to remember or learn something, but to generate new ideas. This is one of the most exciting uses of notes: your notebook becomes a collaborator in the thinking process. Putting thoughts down on paper (or on the screen) gives you fodder for reflection, leading to other ideas that you also capture.

You've experienced this when brainstorming using sticky notes on a whiteboard. Seeing notes on the board suggests other ideas. You move them around to form clusters, suggesting further ideas. A virtuous process follows.

Planning

Many people live by their agendas and bullet journals. When you have many things to do or track—as is often the case when managing long and complex projects—it helps to write things down. Sitting down with a calendar and a sheet of paper will help you plan more effectively than if you had to keep everything in your head.

Imagine you're going on a trip, so you make a checklist of items to pack. Seeing items on the list will remind you of things you may have missed at first. You may also consider the priority of items on the list. (For example, your passport should probably be first.) Visualizing items and the relationships between them helps you prepare for the trip.

Communicating

Although you take most notes for your own sake, you also leave some for others. For example, I sometimes find food containers in our refrigerator with a sticky note that says, "Papa, don't eat!" My kids know that, without this note, their snack might soon be gone. This fits the definition of "brief record," even if it's not meant for "recall." These notes turn your surroundings into shared cognitive environments.

Fidgeting

While writing this book, I asked people on Twitter why they take notes. Bastiaan van Rooden memorably replied, "To slow down the monkey in my head." I can relate: many people pay better attention when their hands are busy. In this case, the primary benefit of scribbling things down is keeping your attention focused; the marks on paper are a nice secondary benefit.

Note-Taking Media

Not only are there many reasons for taking notes, but there are also just as many different ways to do so. You can doodle with a pencil in a notebook, write with a marker on a sticky note, type into an app on your phone, draw with chalk on a sidewalk, or tie a string around your finger. In a pinch, you may even write on your skin.

While walking around Tahoe City, CA, my daughter saw a store she wanted to return to. Lacking paper, she wrote down its name on her hand.

Which is to say, you can make notes from whatever is handy—what matters is catching and preserving fleeting thoughts and observations. That said, it helps to be intentional: different note-taking media are suited for different needs.

Pen and Paper

There are good reasons why paper-based notes remain popular. With a bit of care, paper lasts a long time. Paper requires no batteries, and you don't need a special app or device to read your notes; the paper itself is the medium. Paper is also portable and fast.[1]

But paper also has its downsides. Copying paper-based notes requires specialized equipment (e.g., a photocopier) and lots of time. While notebooks are portable, large paper-based repositories (e.g., collections of notebooks) aren't. You can't search paper or link notes easily to each other. And with bound notebooks, you can only view notes in the order they were written. (Unless they're indexed, which also takes time.)

Here is part of my collection of paper notebooks, spanning two decades. The only way I can find stuff in most of these books is if I know the date when I wrote the note.

---

1. D. M. Levy, *Scrolling Forward: Making Sense of Documents in the Digital Age* (New York: Simon and Schuster, 2001).

Index Cards

Index cards are a convenient way around the constraints of notebooks. Since cards aren't bound together, you can easily re-sort them. They're ideally sized for note-taking: smaller than regular sheets of paper, but large enough to capture a single idea in some detail. And because they use thick stock, they stand up to manipulation.

You can use boxes to keep cards organized. When archived carefully, index cards provide one of the advantages of digital notes: random access. That is, you can jump directly to the note you need without having to flip through the rest. They don't need to be stored in the order they were written; you can archive them alphabetically or in any other organizational scheme.

Because of this flexibility, index cards are a popular thinking medium for researchers and authors who keep and refer to lots of notes. Ryan Holiday, author of several popular books, says that his index card–based note-taking system:

> has totally transformed my process and drastically increased my creative output. It's responsible for helping me publish three books in three years (along with other books I've had the privilege of contributing to), write countless articles published in newspapers and websites, send out my reading recommendations every month, and make all sorts of other work and personal successes possible.

Holiday's system consists of individual index cards with a single thought or quotation on each one. He writes a category label in the top-right corner of each card and stores these cards in one big box. But when working on a specific project, such as a book, he uses a smaller dedicated box for the project.[2] Holiday learned this approach from his mentor, the author Robert Greene. Other authors, such as Vladimir Nabokov, also used index cards to organize their work.[3]

2. https://ryanholiday.net/the-notecard-system-the-key-for-remembering-organizing-and-using-everything-you-read/
3. V. Nabokov, *Strong Opinions* (New York: Vintage, 2001).

Marginalia

Underlining key sentences and writing ideas on book pages is a common way of taking notes while reading. The obvious advantage is that note-taking happens in context: you capture ideas near (or on) the texts that sparked them, so they're easier to understand later. But this is also their main downside: since they don't stand on their own, these notes are harder to reorganize or relate to other notes.

E-books have an edge here. Digital marginalia can be more easily referenced, searched, backed up, and synced. But some people like to mark up physical books with a pen or highlighter. Many of the ideas in Holiday's index cards come from his reading: he annotates books and articles as he reads them, marking passages that stand out and writing thoughts in the margins as he goes along.

Sticky Notes

Personally, I don't like writing in books—but I still want the advantages of taking notes in context. Sticky notes provide a way around this dilemma: I read with a pad of small stickies and a pencil. Whenever I find an idea or passage that resonates, I write a few words on a sticky note and paste it on the book's margins, so it protrudes from the page. In this way, it doubles as a bookmark.

Of course, sticky notes are helpful for more than annotating books. They're also a mainstay of workshops, design studios, and other situations that require groups of people to think together. Using sticky notes, it's easy to turn walls, whiteboards, windows, tabletops, and other ordinary surfaces into temporary placeholders for ideas. (More on this in Chapter 10, where we'll discuss collaborative note-taking.)

Sticky notes' main advantage is that they can be attached and reattached nearly anywhere on a smooth surface. Because of this, they're ideal for exploring relationships between ideas. You can paste notes in any sequence and reorganize them later.[4] That said, larger sticky notes aren't suitable for storing ideas long-term; it's impractical to keep walls and whiteboards covered in notes. (Of course, this doesn't apply to the small sticky notes used to annotate books.)

---

4. A good resource of practices for thinking collaboratively using sticky notes is D. Straker, *Rapid Problem Solving with Post-It® Notes* (Cambridge: Da Capo Lifelong Books, 1997).

Photographs

One way to get around sticky notes' ephemeral nature is to take pictures of the wall or board before taking down the stickies. While photos aren't strictly about making marks, they can be an effective way of capturing ideas and observations. For example, whenever I park in a large, unfamiliar parking lot, I take a photograph of a nearby landmark so that I can find my car later.

I took this photograph in the parking lot of Disney's Animal Kingdom theme park. Note I didn't bother with proper framing; I didn't expect to use this photograph for anything other than finding where I'd parked.

People used cameras as note-taking devices well before personal computers arrived on the scene. Around the mid-Twentieth Century, film-based cameras got small, fast, convenient, and inexpensive enough to serve effectively in this role. In a presentation to shareholders, Polaroid founder Edwin Land described the original (1944) concept for instant photography as

> a kind of photography that would become part of the human being, an adjunct to your memory; something that was always with you, so that when you looked at something, you could, in effect, press a button and have a record of it in its accuracy, its intricacy, its beauty—have that forever.[5]

5. Edwin H. Land in "*The Long Walk*," directed by Bill Warriner, 1970, www.youtube.com/watch?v=zbmq9R0dtVg.

The main advantage of photographing things you want to remember is convenience. You likely have a phone with an excellent camera in your pocket; no note-taking method is faster than taking it out, pointing it at something, and shooting. The obvious downside is that you're limited to capturing what you see in the world—great for remembering where you parked, but less so for recalling abstract ideas.

Audio and Video

One way to remember what you were thinking is to record yourself saying it. Recording equipment used to be fiddly, bulky, and expensive, but smartphones have made recording ubiquitous. Software can transcribe your recordings so you can read and search for what you said.

Recordings are most effective at capturing what somebody says with high fidelity. While you may lose some thoughts when handwriting or typing notes, a recording will capture everything verbatim. This is also its downside: recordings don't benefit from the real-time synthesis you do when using a slower medium. Still, some people love to record themselves "speaking their minds."

Digital Notes

Most of the note-taking means we've highlighted so far existed in some form before computers. But now, we'll focus specifically on digital note-taking. Almost five billion people have a smartphone,[6] and many also use laptop or desktop computers. Most of these devices include note-taking apps, and people use them to write down all sorts of things, ranging from shopping lists to book notes.

Many digital note-taking applications mimic the abilities and superficial characteristics of analog (i.e., "real-world") note-taking media. For example, Macs include an application called *Stickies* that lets you place sticky notes on your computer desktop. Well, not really: Stickies places a series of pixels that *look* like sticky notes on another series of pixels that function like a "desktop."

6. www.statista.com/forecasts/1143723/smartphone-users-in-the-world

How Do You Take Notes?

Throughout this discussion, you may have been thinking about the ways you take notes. Perhaps I missed some on my list; this is your opportunity to set me straight. Make a list of all the media you use to take notes. Don't worry about the order: just write them down as they come to your mind. As you write down each medium, think about what you use it for.

You may use the same medium for different purposes. For example, I use large sticky notes when leaving notes for other members of my family and small sticky notes when bookmarking an idea in a (physical) book. If you run into such cases, write them as separate items on the list. Your list will look something like this:

- Large sticky notes for leaving notes for my family
- Small sticky notes for making notes in books
- Moleskine pocket notebook for taking down ideas on the run
- Whiteboard for keeping track of to-dos
- Etc.

Take a few minutes to make this list and then read the rest of this section. Seriously, put the book down and make the list. No peeking!

OK, you're back. You made the list, right? Good. I'm guessing you might be surprised at how many ways you take notes. We keep track of ideas in many different ways, both analog and digital. You may have half a dozen different sets of notes just on your phone! We'll get this stuff organized soon. For now, just admire the rich variety of ways you have to extend your mind using notes.

One other thing before moving on: I didn't give you explicit instructions about *how* to make the list itself. Where and how did you write it? Did you use pen and paper or your phone or computer? Did you dictate it into a recording device or app? Why did you choose that medium? Hopefully, after reading this chapter, you'll make such choices more intentionally.

These things aren't real in the sense that a whiteboard or paper notebook is real. Instead, software layers metaphors over complex information processing systems. What you see on your computer and smartphone are familiar representations that make it easier for you to work with the device than its native sequences of binary energy states.

Metaphors make new concepts easier to understand by allowing you to use what you already know. Designers use this fact to make applications easier to learn. For example, digital whiteboards simulate physical whiteboards, so your first interactions with such apps are informed by your experience with real-world whiteboards. That said, metaphors aren't perfect: digital notes can do things that physical ones can't. Digital notes let you think differently—but you'll have to leave behind some comfortable metaphors. The main metaphor you'll need to shed is that of a paper notebook organized chronologically or by topic.

Thinking with Things

A theme is becoming clear: notes aren't just a way to extend just your memory but other cognitive abilities as well. It's one thing to write a reminder to buy milk and another to outline a vacation plan. Both call for thinking, but notes help you do them better.

Recent cognitive science research suggests that thinking doesn't happen exclusively in the brain. Instead, we think with our whole bodies as we interact with things and other beings in the world. In *The Extended Mind*, Annie Murphy Paul reviews advances in the field and concludes that intelligence is transactional: "a fluid interaction among our brains, our bodies, our spaces, and our relationships."[7] This is to say that thinking isn't constrained to your nervous system or even to your skin. Things in the world extend and augment your cognition.

In *Figure It Out*, Stephen Anderson and Karl Fast explained that you understand things by interacting with them in the world: you look at things, push-pull-prod-move-etc., add or remove, and otherwise reconfigure. The process reveals possible relationships and patterns—the structure of things as you understand them at the moment.[8]

7. A. M. Paul, *The Extended Mind: The Power of Thinking Outside the Brain* (New York: Eamon Dolan Books, 2021).
8. Stephen P. Anderson and Karl Fast, *Figure It Out: Getting from Information to Understanding* (New York: Two Waves Books, 2020).

Install Obsidian

In the late 2010s and early 2020s, new digital note-taking tools appeared that brought to market capabilities previously available only via specialized software and often in research contexts. Several are worth exploring and investing in. But to make the ideas in this book more tangible, we'll focus on one such tool: *Obsidian*.

Obsidian is a commercial software application created by a small team. As of this writing, it's free for personal use and available on all major desktop and mobile computing platforms. It embodies key principles we'll explore in this book, so it's a great tool for learning. That said, you could use other tools to implement these practices. We'll just focus on Obsidian for illustration.

(If you're already using Obsidian or a comparable note-taking app, feel free to skip the rest of this section.)

To start, download and install Obsidian on your computer or mobile device. If the former, you can install it by visiting https://obsidian.md and following the instructions. If the latter, you can search for Obsidian in your device's app store and install it from there.

Obsidian's first screen gives you several options. If you're using the software for the first time, you can either select Quick Start or Create a new vault. (The other options are mostly for use by existing Obsidian users.)

When you first launch Obsidian, you'll have the choice to create a new vault. In Obsidian, a vault is where you store notes. You can create and manage as many vaults as you want. For example, I currently manage two vaults: one where I manage projects and another that serves as my primary long-term knowledge repository. To use Obsidian, you must create at least one vault.

Under the hood, a vault is simply a folder on your computer containing plain text files. So, if you decide to move on, you can still access your data in a universally compatible format. Go ahead and create your first vault and look around Obsidian's user interface. In the next chapter, you'll create your first note. But for now, just become familiar with the software.

After you create your first vault, Obsidian will open without any note selected. This is understandable since you haven't created anything yet.

Obsidian's user interface has a panel on the left that lists your available notes and a panel on the right that shows the currently open note(s). The parenthetical plural is because Obsidian lets you open several notes simultaneously, which you can view either in tabs or side-by-side.

Think of a typical war movie scene: a ragtag platoon planning an attack. The soldiers huddle close to the ground and, absent paper and pens, draw (literal) lines in the sand and move rocks and twigs to represent targets and units. The commander might say something like, "Hutch, you and Charlie stand here and give cover while Mack and I rush the compound." One soldier might ask a question, and another will contribute an idea—all facilitated by a few rocks and dirt.

The improvised map gets the platoon "on the same page," so to speak. By representing the battlefield as tangible things they can manipulate, they can better think through and communicate their plans, spotting obstacles and opportunities they might miss if they were trying to imagine the situation in their heads. You may have had similar experiences when working with colleagues around a whiteboard.

Once you understand that you think with things, you can explore ways to augment your thinking. The battlefield map and the whiteboard are examples of augmentations that are useful when collaborating with others. Notes are a similar augmentation. As with the whiteboard, you can use them to think collaboratively, but they're also very useful when thinking by yourself.

In *Genius*, his biography of Richard Feynman, James Gleick writes about the role of notes in the physicist's work. Starting from an early age, Feynman worked out problems in his notebooks. Later in life, in an interview with MIT historian Charles Weiner, he explained the role of his notes. Gleick writes,

> He began dating his scientific notes as he worked, something he had never done before. Weiner once remarked casually that his new parton notes represented "a record of the day-to-day work," and Feynman reacted sharply. "I actually did the work on the paper," he said. "Well," Weiner said, "the work was done in your head, but the record of it is still here." "No, it's not a record, not really. It's working. You have to work on paper, and this is the paper. Okay?"[9]

To emphasize the point, notes aren't merely a way to record your thinking; they're part of where thinking happens. They are the means through which you understand and make sense of things. When making notes, you're thinking on the page and beyond, experimenting with temporary models that describe how a part of the world might work. It's a creative, generative act of discovery and clarification.

9. James Gleick, *Genius: The Life and Science of Richard Feynman* (New York: Vintage, 1993).

Gretchen Anderson

Gretchen Anderson is a product consultant, coach, and author based in the San Francisco Bay Area. While working on her book *Mastering Collaboration*, Gretchen built an outline using her computer. She used this outline to think through the high-level ideas in the book. However, the outline became constraining as she got into the details. "I started to lose track of it," she explained. So, she switched to using physical sticky notes:

> I was doing this at home, where I don't have a white-board...But I do have lots of windows, so at one point, I busted out the sticky notes and had the medium-sized ones and one color for chapters and smaller different colored ones for main points and the stories that would buttress them so that I could create that kind of map that I could see all at one time. Interestingly, that happened late in the process, maybe three-quarters of the way through. You know, I was kicking myself like, "Gretchen, you know that you could have done this earlier!"...I probably couldn't have done it any other way. I started out with an outline, I changed that outline to be something that was looser so that I could fit everything I was learning into it, and then I needed to kind of remix it again to make it something that people could follow and not just have it be a laundry list of stuff I learned.[10]

CONTINUES ➤

10. https://theinformed.life/2019/02/03/episode-2-gretchen-anderson/

CONTINUED ➤

By commandeering her walls and windows, Gretchen literally expanded her thinking surface. Moving from an outline to a two-dimensional map of ideas allowed her to see everything at once and "remix" it into a sequence that her readers could follow. Note that she used sticky notes of different colors and sizes, which allowed her to distinguish different structural elements at a glance.

Outlines are great for exploring hierarchical relationships, but not as effective when you want to visualize lots of stuff at the same time. Switching how you're taking down ideas is a common way to get unstuck in complex creative projects. Different media have different capabilities and constraints: it's important to be aware that you might have to switch at some point depending on what you're doing.

Endnotes

As you see, there are many ways of taking notes and many reasons for doing so. But ultimately, you do it to extend your cognitive abilities. Thinking clearly is fundamental to everything you do, so mastering notes will help you in many aspects of your life.

As I mentioned in the introduction, this book focuses on *digital* note-taking. We'll look beyond comfortable metaphors to new means of exploring ideas that are only feasible with computers. You're not building a better Trapper Keeper, but something entirely different and more exciting. But I'm getting ahead of myself. Before you start building your note-taking system, you need to cover a few fundamentals.

2

Make Short Notes

Paper-based media trained you to take monolithic notes: long narrative streams of things you thought and heard. But thinking effectively with digital notes requires that you learn to think and capture information differently. This chapter will show you fundamental distinctions that will help you be more intentional in how and where you take notes.

It starts with becoming aware of how you currently do it and to what ends. Some notes, such as meeting minutes, can have lots of details. Others can be simple scribbles on scraps of paper. None are "right" or "wrong": they all play different roles. For example, when I sat down to write this chapter's introduction, there was a bright pink sticky note on my computer's display. The note said:

> Check out Hugh's thoughts on structure.

I'd written this somewhat cryptic note the day before while reviewing my slides for an upcoming class. As I went over the deck, I realized there was stuff missing. I also remembered a presentation by my colleague Hugh Dubberly that made those points clear. So, I wrote myself a reminder to review Hugh's deck before circling back to my own.

Later, as I clicked through Hugh's slides, I captured ideas using Notability, an app that allows me to take handwritten notes on my iPad. These, too, are notes, but they have a different intent than the sticky note. Rather than remind me of something to do, this second set of notes helped me work out the ideas before revising my presentation.

Both the sticky note and the scribbles in my iPad have limited lifespans. I can toss them once I'm done with my slides. But one of the ideas that emerged from this session seemed worth capturing for the long term, so I added it to my long-term note repository. I didn't have time then to explore the idea's implications, but I could return to it later.

We use the word "note" to describe all of these things, but they serve different needs and take different forms. The sticky note is a handwritten scribble on a piece of paper. The iPad note is also handwritten, but using a digital app. Both are disposable. However, the note in my repository is typed, and I expect to add to it over the years. These are intentional choices.

Write One Note for Each Concept

As you saw in Chapter 1, notes aren't merely marks in the world; they're means for extending your mind. But the medium matters: you think differently depending on *how* you capture ideas. For example, sticky notes lend themselves to taking down one thought per note; you won't outline an entire book by scribbling onto a single sticky note.

Conversely, digital notes are limitless: you could write an entire book on a single note. Given this capability, you may be tempted to capture everything about a subject in a single note. This is a mistake. Instead, aim to make short, focused notes that represent individual concepts.

For example, as you read this book, you might be inclined to capture what you learn in a note. But the point isn't to capture the *book*, it's to learn about the *ideas* in it. An idea might remind you of a similar idea you found in another book. It would be great if you could examine variations in the idea from different perspectives and sources.

So, start a short note for your overall thoughts about the book. But as you come across ideas that matter to you, start separate notes for each. In the next chapter, you'll learn how to link them together. For now, just know that you're aiming for short, focused notes rather than long, comprehensive ones.

WORKING NOTE

Take Note of This

Taking notes helps you remember what you read. Writing down ideas also allows you to "make them your own" by articulating them in your own words and connecting them to other ideas.

Practice by starting a note to capture what you learn in *Duly Noted*. Use Obsidian so you can get a feel for what it's like to take a simple note with the tool. To start a new note, open Obsidian and press CMD-N (or CTRL-N if you're using Windows). You can also go to the File menu and select *New Note*.

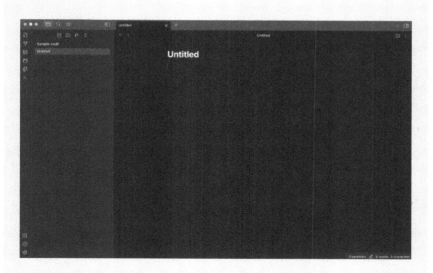

CONTINUES ➤

CONTINUED ➤

Your screen will show a tab with the name *Untitled* and a blinking cursor. Select the word *Untitled* and change it to *Duly Noted*. This will change the file's name to make it easier to find and reference later. After changing the name, press Return (or Enter) on your keyboard to go to the first line of the file.

You can now start writing what you've learned so far. Don't worry about making it perfect. One of the advantages of this way of note-taking is that you can keep coming back to your notes to expand and edit them over time. You just want to get started.

When I take reading notes, I copy the book's chapter structure to help me remember where I found which ideas. For now, you can just write the names of the chapters you've read so far. You can also capture important ideas we've discussed so far. I suggest three lines from the introduction that serve as a summary of the book's approach:

> Make short notes.
>
> Connect your notes.
>
> Nurture your notes.

You can capture these as plain lines in the note. Later, I'll show you how to turn them into links to separate notes about each idea.

(Notice that I tweaked these sentences a bit to make them stand on their own. Specifically, I replaced "them" in the second and third sentences with "notes." When thinking about small, focused notes, consider how they might be understood outside of their original context.)

Essential Distinctions

One of the most effective ways to learn about a subject is to study its distinctions. Every subject has core concepts that play off each other. Once you understand the differences between them, the subject becomes easier to understand. Let's look at four sets of distinctions that are key to effective note-taking.

Note-Taking vs. Note-Making

As you've seen, notes allow you to "spread" your thinking beyond your brain and onto the environment. But not all notes are the same. This one word—"note"—refers to activities, practices, and tools that fulfill different needs. For example, the sticky note on the food container serves a different purpose than the highlights in a book: the first is meant as a message to others ("DON'T EAT!"), while the second is for remembering what you've read. Knowing which sense you mean when you use "notes" can help you think more effectively.

Dr. Fiona McPherson makes a helpful distinction between note-*taking* and note-*making*.[1] Here's my interpretation:

- *Note-taking* is when you take notes to remember what you've heard or read. For example, you may be listening to a professor give a lecture, and you write down the main points to review later. Another example is when you highlight and annotate a book. As you read, some ideas stand out as more important than others, so you underline them or write in the margins to revisit them later.

- *Note-making* is something else entirely: instead of highlighting or capturing ideas from an existing source—a text, lecture, video, etc.—you write down what you're thinking to make sense of your ideas. You've used note-making if you've drawn a mind map or sketched a new arrangement for the furniture in your living room.

I wrote, "you write down what you're thinking," but it's more correct to say that *you think by writing things down*. Thinking isn't just happening in your brain and then captured on paper. Instead, you're thinking *with* and *on* the paper. The scribbles set up a feedback loop: you draw an arrangement that doesn't look quite right but sparks ideas for improvement, so you draw another, and another, and another.

The gist here is that these are different mindsets. You *take* notes to learn and recall but *make* notes to *generate*. Both modalities entail different mindsets and tools. And yet, we use "notes" to refer to both—a semantic quirk that can lead you to make inefficient choices. You can easily take notes using your Kindle's highlighting and annotation features, but that's not the best medium for planning a vacation.

---

1. Fiona M. McPherson, *Effective Notetaking* (New Zealand: Wayz Press, 2012).

Evergreen vs. Transient Notes

As I suggested in the beginning of this chapter, many notes don't have a long shelf life. A grocery list doesn't serve a purpose after you return from the store. We refer to these notes as *transient*: they're useful only for a short time.

But not all notes are like that; some are longer-lived. When reading a book, you might come across an unfamiliar idea you want to learn more about, so you write it down. At first, you won't know much about the subject, so your notes will be sparse and messy. That's okay. As you learn more, you can re-visit the note and add new ideas. Over time, you'll have a comprehensive resource of everything you know about the subject.

Andy Matuschak calls these *evergreen notes*.[2] In contrast to transient notes, evergreen notes remain relevant over time. Matuschak's five principles for writing evergreen notes are an excellent conceptual foundation:

- Evergreen notes should be atomic; that is, each note should focus on one idea.
- They should be concept-oriented, meaning each note should focus on a concept rather than a book, author, project, etc.
- They should be densely linked; that is, they should have lots of links to other notes.
- You should resist the urge to layer on them a top-down structure, since they might be relevant to more than one category.
- You should write them for yourself, not for publication. (Of course, they can serve as the basis for things you publish later.)

The concept of evergreen notes was a revelation to me. As you may recall, I learned to take notes in school as a way to study for exams. Once the exam passed, notes weren't useful to me. That is, I treated all my notes as transient. As a result, I've forgotten a lot of what I learned then. I wasn't incentivized to keep old notes around. Those binders took up a lot of space, and their lack of search facilities made re-finding old ideas challenging.

Obviously, computers make all of this moot. If you organize things with some care, you can easily return to ideas over time to build on them and

---

2. https://notes.andymatuschak.org/

connect them with other ideas. This book focuses primarily on taking and organizing evergreen notes. This isn't to discount the power of transient notes to extend your mind—but the focus here is on learning and making, and evergreen notes are central to that project.

Top-Down vs. Bottom-Up Structures

I want to focus for a bit on Matuschak's fourth principle for taking evergreen notes: the difference between top-down and bottom-up structures. If you're like me, you grew up structuring school notebooks into sections: one for math, one for history, one for social studies, etc. Within sections, notes were stored chronologically (i.e., by date); after each lesson, I'd add new sheets to that section.

This structure worked for school because subjects were clearly defined: there was little overlap between history and biology. Or at least there seemed to be little overlap—in retrospect, there were many interesting connections left unexplored. Drawing strict boundaries between subjects made them seem more disconnected than they really were.

You want to foster connections between ideas. Resist the urge to set up rigid structural distinctions up front. Instead, create schemas that allow for bottom-up structures to emerge. This sounds a bit highfalutin; we'll get to practical recommendations in Chapters 5 and 6. For now, just know that while there is a place for top-down structures in your garden, you want to leave room for future growth.

Present You vs. Future You

The concept of evergreen vs. transient notes implies different uses. But it also implies different time windows. A grocery list is only useful for a little while, whereas you might find value in some evergreen notes throughout your life. But in neither case are you writing things down for "right now." After all, right now the thought—whether buying milk or an interesting new idea—is still in your mind. What you want is to capture that thought so you can recall it later when you need it (for example, at the store or when writing an essay).

As such, you are the audience for many of your notes. But this isn't the you of *now* ("present" you, so to speak), but a future version of yourself, one who's got lots of other things in their mind. This might seem like an esoteric distinction, but it's important to remember you're writing things down for another person. Even if you share lots in common with them, you aren't the same.

The things that seem important to you now might be less relevant to future you. Conversely, *future you* will be more attuned to signals that *present you* misses. One of the points of learning is changing present you into a (hopefully) better future you. When you build a personal knowledge garden, you create possibilities for future you to enjoy a better life based on whatever criteria matters to you. So, strive to make things as clear as possible, regardless of where and when you expect to revisit them.

Minimally Viable Notes

For notes to become an effective means for thinking, you must get into the habit of writing things down quickly. You're not thinking and then writing; you're thinking *as you write.* You'll do it faster if you keep notes simple.

A transient note can be very simple: a few words to jog your memory will do. But evergreen notes require a bit more elaboration. After all, if you come back to the note later, and can't understand what it means, then it won't serve its purpose.

So, you must strike a balance between keeping things as simple as possible while creating enough context to find the note later and understand what it means. Taking a page from product management, I aim to capture *minimally viable notes (MVN)*—i.e., notes that include just enough information not to leave future me hanging.

MVNs provide the key data with enough context to tell you what they're about. Besides a clear name, they often include a call to action, next steps, and a reference to where you came across the idea. Mine include a title, the date of capture, a source reference (e.g., the book where I found the idea), and at least one tag that identifies the note as part of a broader set.

We'll discuss tags in more detail in Chapter 6 and references in Chapter 10. And in Chapter 5, I'll show you how to use templates to automate some of this work. For now, let's focus on writing down the name and date of your note.

Writing with Markdown

As you've seen, Obsidian saves your notes in plain text, the most basic, vanilla file format imaginable. One way to understand plain text is in contrast to the alternative. Most word processors, such as Microsoft Word or Google Docs, allow you to visually style text—i.e., make it *italic*, **bold**, etc. In so doing, they conflate the visual presentation of text with its content.

Plain text files don't include such formatting information. As the name says, they just include the text with no decorations. One advantage of saving information in this format is that plain text has been around for a long time; many applications can open and save files as plain text. The same isn't true for files saved in fancy word processor formats such as DOCX. But, you may protest, you sometimes need styled text. For example, in the first paragraph of this section, I'm calling your attention to italicized and bold text. The paragraph wouldn't work as well if you couldn't see the effects I'm describing. So, there's a tension here: you want a file format that's universally understood, but you also want to be able to style text.

One way around this conflict is to mark up plain text with styling instructions. This entails wrapping words and passages in extra characters that the reader won't see but it conveys styling information for programs that support it. One upside to this approach is that it maintains compatibility while providing additional functionality for users and applications that need it. There are many different ways of marking up text. For example, HTML, which is used to write web pages, is a popular markup language. But HTML isn't useful for note-taking: it's verbose, hard to learn, and error prone.

In response to these issues, developers created simpler markup languages. One such language, Markdown, has been widely adopted.[3]

CONTINUES ➤

---

3. John Gruber created Markdown, with contributions from Aaron Swartz.

CONTINUED ➤

Markdown allows you to achieve many of the same effects that you can achieve with HTML but is much easier to remember and more compact. For example, to italicize a phrase in Markdown, all you need to do is wrap it in asterisks:

Markdown allows you to *emphasize* some text.

If you were to save this sentence in a file and open an editor capable of understanding Markdown, the word "emphasize" would be italicized. As you can see, Markdown has the added advantage that it's understandable even if you open it in an editor that doesn't understand Markdown. It's easy for you to imagine that the two asterisks represent some kind of distinction, even if you don't know exactly what it's meant to be.

Markdown makes basic styling easy. Here are a few conventions to get you started:

```
*italic*
**bold**
# First-level heading
## Second-level heading
### Third-level heading
```

Unordered outline:

```
- Item one
- Item two
- Item three
```

Ordered outline:

```
1. Item one
2. Item two
3. Item three
```

See? It's easy; this is how you'd likely write these things in plain text anyway. And as I said, many note-taking apps use Markdown as their text format.

Naming Your Notes

The most important thing you can do to find your notes later is give them clear titles. When you're browsing through a long list of notes, it's easier to understand what they contain if they have clear titles, such as *Shopping list* or *2022-08-03 Meeting with Claudio*, than if they have generic names such as *Untitled* or *Note 2*. Notes with clear names are also easier to find using your note app's search functionality.

Some note-taking apps, such as Apple Notes, use the first line in the note's text as its title. When you start a new note, the app gives it a generic title (*New Note* in this case). But when you start typing the text of the note, the app replaces this generic title with the first line you've typed into the note. If you change your mind later, you can edit this first line.

Other apps, such as Obsidian and Notion, provide a dedicated title field that is unrelated to the body of the note. This adds a bit more work when writing the note, but it gives you the flexibility of having a title that's independent of the note's text. Some apps also allow you to specify alternative titles, also known as *aliases*, which are useful if you want to link to that note using another name. (More about this in Chapter 3.)

So, note titles are important. But how do you write effective note titles? Here are a few guidelines that will help.

MAKE TITLES DISTINCTIVE

It's important to know what a note is about when looking at its title. This requires that the title clearly differentiate that note from its neighbors. Two contiguous notes called *Meeting* are much more ambiguous than two notes called *2022-08-03 Meeting* and *2022-08-10 Meeting*. Obviously, the key differentiator in this case is the date.

MAKE TITLES SHORT, BUT NOT TOO SHORT

You want to keep your title's word count low so you can easily browse them in lists. But if you make them too short, you might not be able to tell what they're about. I aim for titles that are between three and seven words long. Longer than that, and they'll get truncated in list panels. (This implies keeping key differentiators at the beginning of titles, as in the previous example.)

USE PATTERNS—AND STICK TO THEM

After you've captured notes for a while, you'll notice several notes of the same type: meeting minutes, book annotations, journal entries, etc. You can establish naming patterns to help you identify which is which at a glance. For example, whenever I come across a quote I'd like to keep, I capture it in a note titled *Quote—(first five or so words of the quote)*. This way, whenever that note comes up in another context, I can immediately tell what it's about.

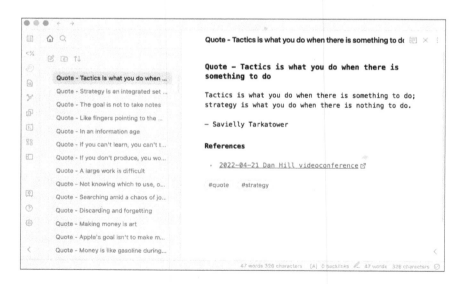

The Best Format for Working with Dates

The date when you captured the note is a surprisingly important bit of information. Later, you may not remember what the note was called, or have only a vague idea of what it was about—but you may know that you came across it in May. So, knowing the capture date can help you find it later.

Note-taking apps add the date and time for you. Paper doesn't. Over the years, I've built the habit of writing the date in the upper-right corner of anything I write on paper, whether in a notebook or a loose sheet of paper. (The exception is sticky notes, since they're often transient or meant to be clustered. When I photograph them, my phone adds the date, time, and location to the picture.)

There are many ways to write dates. You could spell out the month and date (e.g., September 27, 2022) or use numbers and slashes (e.g., 9/27/2022—at least in the U.S.; people in other countries would write 27/9/2022).

Don't bother with any of these. Instead, train yourself to use the ISO-8601 standard format,[4] which consists of numbers representing the year (using four digits), a dash, the month (using two digits), a dash, and the date (using two digits). So, September 27, 2022, would be written as 2022-09-27.

CONTINUES ➤

---

4. www.iso.org/iso-8601-date-and-time-format.html

CONTINUED ➤

While this format may seem awkward at first, it has several advantages. For one, it's compact and consistent: all dates are represented by exactly ten characters. For another, it corresponds to our mental model of the date hierarchy: years contain months which contain days. But more importantly, this format is easier for computers to process. File systems can't easily sort dates written in "human-friendly" formats, whereas the YYYY-MM-DD format is very easy for computers to sort.

While it may be clear why this habit is helpful on computers, you may wonder why I also do it on paper. The simple reason is consistency: it pays to settle on a standard format and use it everywhere. Settling on a standard date format—even if it's one more suited to the computer's constraints than mine—makes it possible for me to retrieve all stuff related to a particular date. But more importantly, it relieves me from having to remember where to use what type of format.

NOTABLE NOTE-TAKER
Sam Ladner

Speaking in an interview on my podcast, design researcher, sociologist, and author Sam Ladner described her approach to capturing what she learns while doing research. When I asked Sam if there was anything we could learn from sociology to improve our productivity, she suggested the concept of "thick description," which I understand to mean adding enough context to our notes so that we know what they refer to. As Sam explained it,

> Thick description doesn't mean writing deeply every single time about every single thing. It's about choosing the things that in the future will have sufficient ambiguity to be meaningless unless you give the context around it. The classic example that Clifford Geertz gave was "the wink." If you see somebody wink, it's not the same as a blink. If somebody blinks, that's an inadvertent movement of the eye. And if you don't have thick description, a wink will, in your notes, just appear exactly the same as a blink. A wink has cultural context, significance, message, a web of significance as Geertz says.[5]

This idea aligns with the concept of a minimally viable note: at first, you want as little content as feasible, but enough to give you context on what the note is about and why it matters. The key question when capturing evergreen notes is: Are you providing enough context for future you to know what this was about? Can you return to this note six months from now and pick back up where you left off?

While taking down a few words now might be expedient, the note won't be of much use if future you can't make sense of it. When writing down a note you expect to revisit in the future, add as many details as necessary to reduce ambiguity—even if it feels like overkill now.

---

5. https://theinformed.life/2022/05/22/episode-88-sam-ladner/

Endnotes

As I finish writing this chapter, the sticky note I mentioned at the beginning is long gone. But the things I learned while revisiting those slides are now captured in my knowledge garden. I expect to revisit them as I learn more.

Knowing which notes to toss and which to keep will make you a better thinker. And knowing how to structure evergreen notes—the minimal amount of information they require—will help you find and understand them when it's time to circle back.

Of course, this assumes that capturing long-term notes is worth your while. Building a knowledge garden takes sustained time and effort, and only you can answer the question "Why am I doing this?" But if your answer involves creating, writing, learning, or any activity that entails intellectual development, read on.

In this chapter, we examined one essential component of knowledge gardens: short, focused notes. In the next chapter, we'll look at the second essential component: links between those notes.

CHAPTER

3

Connect Your Notes

Short, focused notes are essential to a productive knowledge garden. But these atomic notes don't do much good on their own. Their power only becomes evident when you link them together.

Linking allows you to go deeper into individual ideas without losing the connection to their original context. It also enables you to discover connections to other relevant contexts and ideas. Thinking in terms of granular, linked ideas will nudge you to broaden your understanding and spark unexpected insights.

Ideas come through various means, sometimes serendipitously. They often spur other ideas—although how they fit together might not be clear at first. During capture, you can't organize them into the best possible order. In fact, there might not be a "best" order at all: one idea might apply to several contexts.

Premature organization limits information's usefulness. But you don't have to commit to an organization scheme up front. Digital note-taking enables you to organize ideas freely so you can find multiple, different paths to knowledge.

Consider how Wikipedia works. Each page includes links to other pages. There isn't a definitive set of folders or top-down categories; instead, each page is part of a network of interrelated ideas. You're aiming for a similar structure with your notes.

A typical Wikipedia page. The blue text represents links to other pages in the system, which are peers to this one. This page isn't stored in a top-down container but is instead part of a network of interlinked pages.

Hypertext Note-Taking

Wikipedia is an example of a hypertext: a collection of information where ideas link to other ideas nonlinearly. That is, you don't read the material from beginning to end in a straight sequence. Instead, you jump around from one idea to another by clicking (or tapping) on links that take you to related ideas. There's order there, but it's bottom-up.

Like Wikipedia, hypertext note-taking systems allow for order to emerge spontaneously as you link notes. The result is a complex link-node graph connecting ideas to other ideas. Any one note can serve as the starting point of a particular exploration: the more notes, the broader the possibilities.

This isn't a new idea. In 1945, Vannevar Bush published "As We May Think," an influential article that argued for nonlinear information management systems.[1] Ted Nelson coined the word *hypertext* in 1965, framing it as a means for dealing with complex sets of interrelated information that could be elaborated and annotated.[2]

Current hypertext note-taking apps, such as Roam, Obsidian, and Notion, bring these theoretical visions to practical use. These and other hypertext note-taking tools allow you to explore ideas in their original context (e.g., the project through which they found you) and independently of that context, so you can remix and reuse them later.

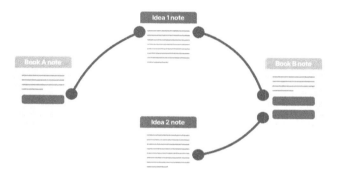

Keeping ideas separate while linking them to each other gives you the best of both worlds: the ability to revisit ideas in their original context and explore them from different perspectives. Capturing atomic, linked notes also allows you to delegate some of the relationship-building to computers: with a bit of up-front structure, your computer can find new connections.

Additionally, hypertexts evolve. You can revisit notes as you learn more about the ideas they capture. When you do, you get new ideas. The result is more of a living network than a notebook. As Nelson put it, "Such a system could grow indefinitely, gradually including more and more of the world's written knowledge."[3] It's a powerful approach to learning and creating.

1. Vannevar Bush, "As We May Think," *The Atlantic Monthly* 176, no. 1 (1945): 101–108.
2. Ted H. Nelson, "Complex Information Processing: A File Structure for the Complex, the Changing and the Indeterminate," *ACM '65: Proceedings of the 1965 20th National Conference*, August 1965, 84–100.
3. Idem

Should You Change Apps?

Most popular note-taking apps allow you to add links. But many make the process cumbersome, which slows down your thinking.

In most cases, linking with these "traditional" apps involves selecting a string of text and pressing an "Insert link" button. (Or its equivalent; the feature's exact name will be different in different apps.) After clicking the button, the app prompts you to enter the destination address. When you paste the address and press "Apply" (or equivalent), the text string becomes a link.

Adding a link in Evernote, a popular cloud-based note-taking app. As with many traditional note-taking apps, this is a multistep process that requires pressing a dedicated "Insert link" button and filling out a small form.

While the "insert link" functionality is widespread, it doesn't work the same everywhere. Links are more central to some apps than others. Some apps require multiple steps to create a link. Also, many assume links are *external*—i.e., pointing outside the note-taking app.

When building a knowledge garden, you want to easily and quickly make links on-the-fly—especially to other notes in the system. So, while you *could* build a hypertext using traditional note-taking apps, many don't make it easy.[4] If your current app makes linking difficult, switch to one that makes links a core feature.

4. This section was last revised in June 2023 and refers to the versions of these applications available then. When you read this, these apps may support more efficient linking to other notes in the app; check with their vendors.

Links and Nodes: The Basic Elements of Hypertexts

At their most basic, hypertexts are composed of nodes (ideas, texts, images, videos, etc.) and links between them. It's worth digging deeper into both of these concepts. In its broader sense, a link relates one thing to another. For example, you're linked to your relatives through familial bonds. But in this book, we're discussing a very particular type of link: *hyperlinks*.

A *hyperlink* is a formal connection between one item in a hypertext and another item. These connections have an origin and a destination. The origin is often a word or phrase, and the destination is another document, note, web page, etc. This pattern is familiar to you from the web.

Like Wikipedia, hypertext note-taking apps let you make links in your notes. Links can point to other notes in the app or any resource that provides a Uniform Resource Identifier (URI), the addressing scheme used on the web. For example, to link to the Wikipedia page about hypertext, you'd use the following URI:

https://en.wikipedia.org/wiki/Hypertext

Nodes refer to the origin and destination objects (pages, documents, notes, or whatever) that are joined by links. Nodes and links are the yin and yang of hypertext systems: you can't have one without the other. Their joint presence is what defines a hypertext.

As suggested previously, nodes can take many forms. A web page can be a node and so can a note in your note-taking app. Images, video, or audio files can also be nodes. Some note-taking apps also allow you to link to specific sections of notes, such as paragraphs. These more granular destinations are known in systems like Obsidian and Roam as *blocks*.

But Can You Do It Using Paper?

While computers are a natural medium for capturing ideas as graphs of linked nodes, you can also do it by using pen and paper. It's just not as practical. People have built elaborate paper-based systems using index cards with unique identifiers.

The downsides are obvious. Storing a large amount of paper requires lots of space. There's also the cost and clutter of dedicated furniture and writing materials. Also, such systems are difficult to back up and not portable.

But more importantly, paper-based hypertexts place the onus of enacting links on you. You must carefully write the correct address on each card and always store them in the expected location. And since you must follow connections manually, paper-based hypertexts are much slower. And, of course, you can't search paper-based hypertexts.

So, yes, you could build a hypertext note-taking system using paper. Others have done it successfully. But you must understand the downsides: it's slow, inconvenient, bulky, costly, and relatively fragile.

So, digital it is. But what *kind* of digital? After all, there are lots of note-taking apps. Some have been around for a long time, and many allow you to create links. Why are we talking about linking now as though it's something new? The short answer is that apps such as Roam Research, Obsidian, Logseq, and Notion make linking much easier.

Linking in many note-taking apps is a multistep process: you type a text, select part of it, go to a menu or toolbar, press a button, and then fill out a short form that includes the link address and name. And in some cases, you can't easily add links to other notes, only to external URIs.

Rather than a rare operation to be accommodated occasionally, hypertext-oriented note-taking apps assume linking is central to the note-taking process. As a result, they make it easy to create links *while writing*—i.e., without lifting your fingers off the keyboard to hunt around for menus or toolbars or having to fill out forms. You can also easily point to other notes in the system.

Add Links to Your Notes

Many hypertext note-taking apps, such as Obsidian, Notion, Roam, and Logseq, include a feature called *wikilinks* that lets you link to existing or new notes as you type. It's simple: all you do is enclose a word or phrase in double brackets, like so:

[[Note two]]

When you do this, the app looks for a note called *Note two* in the system. If there is one, the text *Note two* becomes a link to that note. If there isn't a note with that name, the app will create one for you when you click on the link. This works whether you type double brackets around an existing phrase or when typing a new one: when you type the second closing bracket, the app looks for a match.

For this to work, the phrase must match the note's title *exactly*—i.e., the same sequence of characters must be present in both. Some apps treat uppercase and lowercase characters differently, so [[Note two]] and [[note two]] point to different notes. That said, many apps auto-complete the link's name from existing note titles, which makes linking easier and more consistent.

Try it now. Revisit the note you started to capture ideas about this book and go to the phrase Connect notes to other notes. Now type two left brackets before the word Connect and two right brackets after notes., like so:

[[Connect notes to other notes.]]

When you finish typing the two right brackets, the entire sentence will change color, signifying that it's now a link. But it's not yet pointing anywhere, since you don't have a note with that name in your system. When you click on this link, Obsidian will create a new note called Connect notes to other notes. You can edit it separately from the original note. But notice that if you change the second note's name, the name of the link in the first note will change as well.

Types of Links

You're familiar with how web links work. But there's more to links than what you see online. Just as there can be many types of nodes, there are different types of links. Modern hypertext note-taking apps support more than just simple wikilinks. As these systems become more popular, you must expand your understanding of links.

Let's recap how links work on the web:

- Web links are defined by a document's author.
- They can originate from words, phrases, or images (such as icons).
- Destinations can be anything a web browser can display and can be located with a URI.
- Clicking on a link loads the destination document in your browser.
- This is a one-way jump: while you can click the browser's "back" button to go back a step, most web pages don't have explicit links pointing back to the originating document.

The simplicity of this scheme contributed to the web's popularity, since it's easy to learn for both authors and readers. However, hypertext researchers have explored several other types of links since the late 1960s. Some are now available in hypertext note-taking apps such as Roam Research, Obsidian, and Logseq. Here are seven you should know about:

Wikilinks

We've already covered these, but they're worth calling out since they are central to how these apps work. Wikilinks are like web links in that you select a word or phrase and point it to another note (or any asset you can access through a URI). The difference is that wikilinks are easier and faster to use, resulting in a more fluid linking process.

Implicit Links

Unlike web links or wikilinks, implicit links aren't intentionally defined by the author. Instead, the system creates them based on metadata such as a note's title or creation date. For example, Obsidian lets you see notes that include a phrase that matches your current note's title. (Obsidian calls these *unlinked mentions*.)

For example, you may have a note that includes the phrase "Duly Noted" that isn't a link. If you have another note called *Duly Noted*, your app treats the phrase as though it was a link to that note, since it matches its name exactly.

Backlinks

When discussing traditional web links, I said web pages don't explicitly link back to the originating document. But many modern hypertext note-taking tools let you see lists of all the notes that have links pointing to the note you're currently examining. These "backlinks" make it easy for you to discover relationships between notes, even if they are defined by one-way links.

A note in Roam Research shows "5 Linked References" at the bottom—i.e., backlinks from other notes that point to this one.

Block References

Block references are explicit links, but instead of pointing to a whole document or note, they point to blocks (e.g., individual paragraphs or sections) within the destination. It's worth noting that HTML (the markup language of the web) supports block references. You've experienced them when you've clicked on a link in a web page that takes you to a different part of that page.

Aliases

These are pointers to the original item—sometimes with an alternate spelling—that "stand in" for the original in other places such as lists, folders and other notes. While they appear and behave like the original, they're placeholders that merely represent the original in a separate context. That way, you can have what seems like an instance of a note, document, or item in more than one parent container.

Some apps (including Obsidian) also allow you to define alternate names for notes, so you can link to them using different phrases. For example, you could define the word Hypertext as an alias of the note called Connect notes to other notes. That way, when you use the word Hypertext as a link, it will point to that note. While not technically links, these types of aliases provide a different way of relating notes by giving them alternative names.

Embeddings

I mentioned that clicking on a web link replaces what you're looking at in the browser with the destination document. But embeddings (or "transclusions") are something else entirely. Rather than "taking you" to the destination document, an embedding inserts the destination's content (whether an entire note or a block) into the body of the originating note. Changes to the destination are reflected in the embedded version.

Spatial Relations

All the links I've described so far appear within documents such as notes or web pages. But you can also define relationships by laying out notes on a map and moving some closer to others. Proximity suggests connections; you can relate ideas by clustering them. You've used spatial relations when working with whiteboard tools such as Mural, Miro, and FigJam. Obsidian itself includes a feature called *Canvas* that lets you define spatial relations between notes. All of these tools let you build affinity maps of ideas that are like spatial hypertexts.

Block Links and Embeddings

Sometimes you don't want to link to a note but to an individual paragraph. This is especially useful when referencing information in long notes. In Obsidian, you do this by typing an up carat (^) inside double brackets, like this:

[[^]]

When you type these characters, the app shows a drop-down that lets you pick a block (or paragraph) within the current note. If you type two carats rather than one, you can search for any block in your vault. You can also link to blocks in other notes. To do this, you type the note's name before the up carat:

[[Some title^]]

When you type this character, Obsidian shows a drop-down selector that presents each paragraph in the destination note. You then click on the paragraph you want. The link changes to include a number, like this:

[[Some title#^1f4785]]

This code is a reference to that particular paragraph (or block) in the destination note. If you click on the link, you'll go to that location in the destination note with that block highlighted. You can customize these reference names to make them more readable.

Introduction

Traditionally, we've been told to use our heads. But this injunction gets things backwards — we use our heads too much. The role of the brain had been oversold — what Andy Clark described as "brainbound" thinking. This is what can be thought of as "neurocentric bias."

![[Quote - The brain as the most wonderful organ in my body#^|]]

Quote - The brain as the most wonderful organ in my body

I used to think that the brain was the most wonderful organ in my body. Then I realized who was telling me this.— Emo Philips
965991

Ye   #quote

th

Type # to link heading   Type ^ to link blocks   Type | to change display text

We've used several analogies and metaphors to think about the brain. Two prominent (and surprisingly old) ones:

Embedding a note in Obsidian.

While it's very useful to be able to link directly to paragraphs, it would be even more useful if you could include the paragraph itself within the body of the origin note. This is called *embedding*. To embed a note within another note in Obsidian, you add an exclamation point before the opening brackets, like so:

!
[[Some title#^1f4785]]

One of the upsides of this approach is that changes to the destination note will be reflected in the embedded note. This works both for blocks within notes and entire notes (i.e., you don't need to include the carat reference to a paragraph to embed one note into another).

Tips for Effective Hypertext Note-Taking

Hypertexts change your relationship to knowledge. But working in this way requires re-thinking your relationship with notes. Before moving on, I'll leave you with three tips to keep in mind when taking hypertext notes.

Make Notes Modular

As mentioned previously, notes work best when each note explores one idea. Resist the urge to lump everything into one note; make short, focused notes instead.

For example, if you're reading a book about African fauna, you'll learn about many different animals. Rather than starting a long note to capture everything, create a separate note for each kind of animal. You can also create a note called *Animals of East Africa* where you list—and link—the various animals you read about.

Some things you learn about a species merit their own notes. For example, you may note that hippopotamuses are mammals. Rather than write about mammals in the note about hippos, you can link to a separate note where you explore mammals. Later, if you learn about other mammals such as elephants, you simply link to the existing note about mammals.

Rewire Yourself to Link During Capture

One of the hardest things about hypertext note-taking is getting used to the idea that you're not writing a single monolithic note but a set of related notes. As you start typing your central idea, related ideas might occur to you. Rather than typing them out then and there, you can start a separate note by linking to it inline.

Don't write down the whole idea then and there. Instead, type the left double brackets to start a wikilink. Then you can quickly click to the new note to capture that thought in a separate—but now linked—note. With time, doing this will become second nature.

Use Aliases for Cleaner Links

As you've seen, wikilinks require that you type the note's *exact* title. Because of this, a link called Hypertext points to a different note than a link called hypertext. This is confusing, since they both refer to the same concept; the only difference is the capitalization of the first letter.

Apps let you define alternate labels for links, but this adds friction to the process. Instead, define aliases to notes that you expect to call up by using different names. In this case, you could specify that Hypertext, Hypertexts, hypertext, and hypertexts all point to the same note. That way, the link works correctly when used in a variety of different sentences.

NOTABLE NOTE-TAKER
Jerry Michalski

Jerry Michalski is a futurist and consultant. In 1997, he began using a hypertext tool called TheBrain to capture and connect ideas in a system that he calls *Jerry's Brain*. As of this writing, Jerry's Brain contains over half a million entries: small notes representing different concepts he's encountered over the years. These concepts link to other concepts, forming complex networks. In an interview with NPR, Jerry said,

> It's sort of like Photoshop for ideas. It's a good tool for drawing or for putting things down in context and linking them to each other. Beyond that, it doesn't do very much.[5]

CONTINUES ➤

5. www.capeandislands.org/show/living-lab-radio-on-cai/2017-09-18/
jerrys-brain-the-online-version-has-been-going-strong-for-20-years#stream/0

CONTINUED ➤

What it does do is serve as an external memory—a sort of personal Google consisting solely of ideas and connections curated by Jerry. But Jerry's Brain isn't just good for remembering. Instead, it's shifted how he thinks about things in general. In an interview on my podcast, he described how using the system has changed how he thinks:

> One of the things I love about curating TheBrain is that daily I'm thrust into [Daniel Kahneman's] System Two thinking of: is this worth remembering? If so, what is it? Where do I put it? Because I don't have any orphan thoughts in my Brain—at least not intentionally—everything is hooked like a Christmas ornament onto some branch. And then it's like, "Okay, so what do I call it? What is it connected to? What can I learn from it?"
>
> And then I'll google the thing some more, and then I'll weave a little bit. And so, I'm always doing this little bit of contextual weaving all over the place a little at a time with no particular order. It's extremely random. It's as life hits me, kind of, or as the task I set forth for the day or whatever. So, when you and I have this podcast, I had set up a node—a thought—for this podcast, and I went back to it where I had connected it to the document you sent me for prep, to you, I've got you in context, and I put you in a long time ago. So, that just refreshes my wet brain immediately, and I can step into the conversation like I'm stepping into a stream.[6]

6. https://theinformed.life/2023/04/23/episode-112-jerry-michalski/

This sounds close to the type of hypertextual thinking described by Ted Nelson in the mid-1960s.

TheBrain presents thoughts in a visual canvas where position matters: some represent parent-child relationships while others are siblings. Navigating between them is easy, allowing you to discover new connections between thougths. Yes, you: Jerry's Brain is available via web browsers and is open for anyone to peruse. In that way, it's more than a personal memory: it's also a public one. You can explore Jerry's Brain at www.jerrysbrain.com.

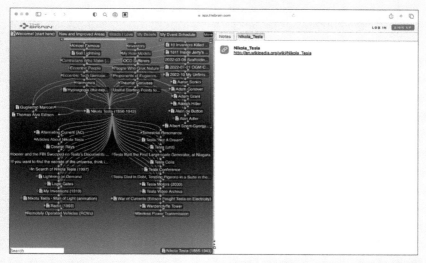

A thought rendered in Jerry's Brain.

Endnotes

As you saw in previous chapters, tools are extensions of your mind. You think more effectively using the right tools, and those used traditionally to organize and manage information—linear notebooks divided into top-down categories—don't cut it in our ever-more complex world.

Hypertexts allow you to find new paths to knowledge that better meet modern information management needs. Structurally, they're set up for thinking in systems, allowing you to track down root causes of problems, see new opportunities, uncover relationships, and manage information overload. As a result, connected notes are the right tool for sense-making in a fast-changing, complex world.

But hypertext note-taking requires different skills than previous media. You must become adept at conceptualizing ideas more granularly and considering how they might link to other ideas. Note names and metadata become more important as you establish ways for new organization patterns to emerge from the bottom up. And you must give up the idea of a one "right" order to information.

But it's doable—and worthwhile. If note-taking is about extending your cognitive abilities, hypertext notes represent the most powerful means for extension that has yet been devised. When managed skillfully, connected notes will spark insights and make you more productive.

4

Plan for a Knowledge Garden

You'll only tap into the power of connected notes when you approach them as components in a system. Its goal: helping you think better.

Carpenters work best when they have the right tools and materials when they need them. Their workshops provide focus, shelter, ventilation, and lighting, among other things. Carpenters configure these places to make their jobs easier. The right mix of tools, processes, and place enable states of mind conducive to good work.

You, too, must make space for good work. By "space," I don't necessarily mean a physical space (although it helps to have a quiet place to work). Instead, I mean a collection of tools and processes that support your work and which you can "go into" to do focused work.

I think of it as a garden, but I'm not the first to use this metaphor in this space. People have associated digital note-taking with gardening and farming since at least the early 1990s.[1] The image is fruitful (sorry!) because gardening shares important characteristics with knowledge management:

- Like seeds, ideas start small and bloom if given proper care.
- Like plants, stewarding ideas takes sustained, disciplined effort.
- Both efforts create nourishment, pleasure, satisfaction, and fulfillment.
- Neither is fully under your control; both types of gardens have lives of their own, and the best you can do is set up structures that allow things to grow organically and then tend to them.

You likely already use several note-taking tools and processes, but haphazardly. In this chapter, we'll bring them together as a coherent system that supports your work. Let's start by looking at what you currently have.

A Process for Thinking with Notes

The best way to think about the system's components is to lay them out according to the role they play in one of six sequential stages. They are the following:

1. Notice
2. Capture
3. Sort
4. Retain
5. Nurture
6. Share

Each stage calls for different tools, workflows, practices, and mindsets. Some, such as noticing and capturing, must be done on-the-fly, often under distracting conditions. Others, such as nurturing and sharing, require more focus and reflection. Let's look at them in more detail. Later, we'll devote whole chapters to some of these.

---

1. During an interview in my podcast, longtime hypertext researcher and software designer Mark Bernstein attributed an early use of the metaphor to Cathy Marshall at Xerox PARC. https://theinformed.life/2022/10/23/episode-99-mark-bernstein/

Take Stock of Your Note-Taking Tools

You likely take notes in various ways: sticky note reminders, a bound notebook for meeting minutes, underlining and annotating books, shopping lists in your phone's notes app, etc. Before configuring your ideal knowledge garden, it helps to make an inventory of all the ways you take notes.

Using a blank sheet of paper (or a spreadsheet on your computer), make a table with three columns:

- **Column 1:** A way to take notes (e.g., Notes app)
- **Column 2:** What you use it for (e.g., shopping list)
- **Column 3:** Whether those uses are evergreen or not

Each note-taking medium may serve more than one purpose. For example, you may use your Notes app to write shopping lists *and* the names of books you want to read later. If so, make a new entry in the table for each separate purpose.

Conversely, you may use more than one medium for the same purpose. For example, sometimes you may write shopping lists on slips of paper in addition to your Notes app. In those cases, too, make a new entry in the table. It will look something like this:

MEDIUM	PURPOSE	EVERGREEN?
Stickies	Reminders	No
Notes app	Shopping lists	No
Notes app	Books to read	Yes
Paper slips	Shopping lists	No

CONTINUES ➤

CONTINUED ➤

Set aside at least fifteen minutes to make this list. Aim to capture the most important media and purposes (i.e., those which play key roles in your life). If you're at home or in your office, look around you to see if you might have forgotten anything. Open your phone and computer and look through your applications. Are you taking notes using any of them? Write them down.

Keep this list present as you explore the plan for your knowledge garden. You'll want to pay special attention to evergreen notes, since those will need to find a special place in your system.

Notice

A good system for thinking starts with understanding how your mind works: how it notices things and comes up with new ideas. As you saw earlier, it's not just about what happens inside your head: your context (for example, your environment and things and other beings in it) influences your thinking.

As you go through your day, you interact with things and people that spark ideas. Perhaps you receive an email that reminds you to renew your car's registration, have an informal conversation with a colleague that answers a long-standing question, or see a review for an interesting new book. Some of these things might be worth revisiting; others won't.

You must hone your ability to focus on things that matter. Not everything is worth noting. A phone number might be a keeper, but what about that original tune you're humming? If you're a musician, the tune could turn into a hit single. In that case, you should take it down. If not, the tune might be a trifle; it may be best to let it go.

How do you hone your attention? It's not enough to read about it: understanding the mind requires observing it. There are several ways you can practice becoming more attentive:

- **Configure your devices to respect your attention.** The easiest thing you can do is mute your notifications. Most of the messages you get on your phone can wait.

- **Set aside times of the day as regular "quiet time."** I wrote the bulk of this book between 5 and 7 in the morning, before most other members of my household were awake.
- **Learn to meditate.** Meditation is the best means I've found to observe my mind. Among its many advantages, meditation makes you more aware of your state of attention in a variety of contexts.

However you do it, noticing what's going on with your mind—and learning to distinguish trivial stuff from stuff worth keeping—is the first stage in the process. Keep distractions at bay and practice paying attention to what's happening around you.

Capture

If you've developed awareness of how your mind works, you'll recognize its fleeting nature. You repeat that new phone number to yourself over and over again, and still—poof, it's gone! So, the next step is to capture your thoughts and observations.

Capture must happen close to noticing, lest the thought slip away. Ideally, you have pen and paper to take down that phone number shortly after you hear it. This requires preparation (e.g., remembering to pack a pen and pocket notebook). And, of course, you can also use your phone to write a note, snap a photo, or record a short audio snippet.

This practice still requires knowing where to capture different types of thoughts. You might dictate a phone number into the voice memo app on your phone, but snapping a photo might not be as useful. Some ideas can be captured in text; others must be doodled. A tune might be hummed.

Whatever the case, you must develop the habit of capturing thoughts at the moment—and determining the best way of doing so—without thinking too much about it. In the next chapter, we'll go into more detail on how to capture ideas effectively.

For now, remember that the process of externalizing your thoughts onto things in the world—notebooks, marginal notes, audio recorders, etc.—spurs further ideas. A feedback cycle ensues whereby your note-taking medium becomes an extension of your mind.

Sort

If you're constantly capturing your thoughts, you'll soon have lots of notes all over the place. You may have more than one app, several paper notebooks, sticky notes, loose sheets of paper, etc. At this point, you've freed your mind from remembering these ideas, but you're burdened with remembering where everything is stored.

If you're using paper, you may have a physical inbox where you pile stuff to be processed. Most note-taking apps also have the digital equivalent of an inbox: a running list of the latest thoughts you've captured. Many people keep their notes in such running lists, but that makes it harder to find stuff later.

My inboxes in three separate note-taking apps. Every once in a while, I go through these notes to either toss them or move them to more permanent locations.

So, the next step in the process is organizing your notes. Some notes will be reminders to take some action in the future, in which case they should go into your "to do" management app.[2] As we discussed previously, some notes you'll keep for later reference, while others you can toss. In Chapter 6, we'll cover organizing and triaging your notes.

---

2. An excellent resource for learning to do this is David Allen's *Getting Things Done*. David Allen, *Getting Things Done: The Art of Stress-Free Productivity* (New York: Penguin, 2015).

Retain

You can keep transient notes where they are or delete them if they've served their purpose. But you want to save the evergreen stuff. The goal of this step is getting worthwhile ideas into a trusted repository where you can find them later. With a bit of foresight, you'll also create conditions for ideas to connect with other ideas down the line.

While you can capture notes directly into your repository, it's likely you'll use separate apps for these purposes. For example, I save contact information (such as phone numbers and email addresses) in Daylite, a customer relationship management (CRM) application, but I save meeting minutes in Obsidian. Each app has characteristics that make them optimal for these use cases. And since I'm disciplined about where I store different types of information, I don't have to think about where to look for specific things later.

Nurture

After some time of saving notes into trusted repositories, you'll have a large collection. Some will have specific uses, such as people's contact details. Others might be useful in many other contexts. For example, you may learn a new concept that becomes an essential part of how you approach your work. The note for this concept could become evergreen, which means that you add to it as you learn more information over time.

You want to be able to revisit these notes so you can recombine and recontextualize them to produce new ideas. Whatever new ideas emerge from revisiting evergreen notes also go into the repository. By connecting notes, you develop a network of ideas that expands the scope of your thinking.

This is where computers shine. Every prior stage in the process can be done using paper, if a bit less conveniently. But digital note-taking systems allow you to link ideas faster and more conveniently than any other medium. And with AI, computers can identify relationships you might have missed. We'll learn more about the nurturing stage of the process in Chapters 6 and 7 and using AI in Chapter 10.

Share

You can share what you learn via blog posts, videos, tweets, presentations, workshops, books, online courses, etc. To further the garden metaphor, these are the "fruits" of your work: ideas that (hopefully) add to the world's store of knowledge or beauty.

One of the wonderful (and scary!) things about sharing your thoughts is that it exposes you to other ideas. People will correct you where you're wrong, suggest books you might have missed, or simply talk about ideas they're passionate about. This feedback can generate new ideas—new seeds for your garden.

You can set things up to make it easier to create new things from what you've learned and thought—the connections you've made between ideas—and to integrate the feedback you get from others. Chapter 8 focuses on this stage of the process.

A Model Knowledge Garden

Let's review the whole process in the diagram below:

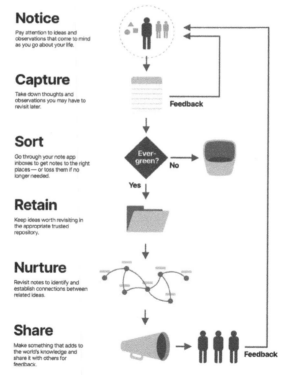

This diagram serves as a plan for your knowledge garden. Each stage calls for different tools, techniques, and practices.

Let's begin with noticing. As I mentioned earlier, you can turn off notifications on your devices. There are also mindfulness and meditation apps that can help hone your attention. (I use one called *Waking Up*.[3]) You can also use an app like Readwise to prompt you with ideas, quotes, and flashcards.

Capturing information entails having tools on hand to take down thoughts. It could be a slim pocket notebook and pen or a note-taking app on your phone. Depending on what you're trying to capture, it could be a camera or audio recorder. More likely, you'll capture thoughts with a combination of apps and tools.

This leads to thoughts and data spread out over different apps, notebooks, devices, and more. That's risky—you may have externalized the thought, but now you need to remember where you stored it. To avoid this, set up inboxes to consolidate these notes.

You're already using inboxes. You may have a physical inbox in your home for paper bills and other correspondence. But the most obvious analog is your email inbox. If you have only one email address, you'll have one place where you check for new messages. (Consider yourself lucky!) But you'll likely have more than one.

I use Apple's Mail app because it aggregates all my incoming emails into a "unified" inbox. I know that any email sent to me will be there. Every day, I go through this inbox to sort my emails. Some are for information only. Some require action on my part. Some are responses to requests I've made of others.

They don't stay in my inbox long. I sort them into appropriate containers depending on what needs to happen next. Some go into project folders on my computer, others are turned into tasks in my task manager app, and others into appointments in my calendar.[4]

The unified list of emails is one of several inboxes I triage during the day. I do something similar with DEVONthink, a database application I use to save web bookmarks, PDFs, and more.[5] Whenever I read something that might be relevant for a project (e.g., my newsletter or this book), I save it to DEVONthink. These items show up in DEVONthink's inbox, where I can tag them and move them to different folders. I do this weekly.

---

3. www.wakingup.com
4. For more on triaging your inboxes, see Allen (2015).
5. www.devontechnologies.com/apps/devonthink

It's easy to go overboard with this stuff. Many of these apps have their own inboxes, so you could end up with a bunch of inboxes you must trawl through to stay organized. One of my operating principles is to reduce the number of inboxes. I do this by configuring my capture apps to save (or copy) new notes or documents into an "everything bucket" application. (In my case, that's DEVONthink.)

This includes notes I take on paper. Whenever I jot something down on a physical notebook, I photograph it with an app called *Scanner Pro* that saves them as PDFs in Dropbox. From there, they go into my DEVONthink inbox. Setting up this workflow took some up-front work. But in practice, I seldom have to think about it. I know my DEVONthink inbox will have the latest items from these apps. From there, I can organize and triage them much like I do my email.

DEVONthink is also my primary knowledge store. This is where most of my content awaits re-discovery. For example, I have a folder where I save articles and posts I've found online and another where I keep PDFs of papers from journals and other academic publications. DEVONthink also indexes my evergreen notes in Obsidian.

When I'm working on a blog post or presentation, I go into this repository and search for content related to whatever I'm writing about. My work at this stage consists of identifying connections between ideas, looking for gaps in my understanding, finding relevant tangents, etc.

The process is aided by my foresight in tagging content items and DEVONthink's AI features. New ideas and research materials emerge from the synthesis work. These go back into the system, becoming fodder for future work. Sometimes, these new connections prompt ideas for new posts—a bottom-up approach to the work.

Doing this type of generative thinking with computers has obvious benefits. Apps have much better search and linking capabilities than paper. Many also allow you to visualize information in different ways, switching between outline views, maps, and other representations. You can explore different configurations, save snapshots, roll back changes, and jump to linked ideas. In short, using computers to steward and develop ideas extends your cognitive abilities in powerful new ways.

You can also quickly share what you're learning by publishing blog posts, posting to social media, sending newsletters, and more. For example, while writing this book, I shared early drafts of sections via my blog and newsletter. I often received useful comments that changed how I think about the material.

The point is that working with ideas is a multistep process, and each step calls for different tools and techniques. Your knowledge garden won't be a single tool but a set of tools that work in concert to enable your thinking. It's easier if the tools work well together so we'll look at three principles to ensure that your garden can work as a whole. But first, let's look at the work of a master knowledge manager.

NOTABLE NOTE-TAKER
Niklas Luhmann

Photo by Universitätsarchiv St.Gallen | HSGH 022/000941 | CC-BY-SA 4.0, CC BY-SA 4.0, via Wikimedia Commons https://commons.wikimedia.org/w/index.php?curid=125616346

Niklas Luhmann (1927–1998) was a German sociologist and academic. Over his career, Luhmann published over 70 books and nearly 400 academic papers on subjects ranging from law to love. His work has been influential in several fields.

The key to Luhmann's prodigious productivity was his use of a *zettelkasten*,[6] a note-taking system based on index cards and filing cabinets. Whenever he came across an important idea, he would note it on a slip of paper about the size of an index card, one per idea. Using an elaborate addressing scheme, he'd write references to other slips that contained related ideas. Luhmann stored the slips in large cabinets in an order that reflected each note's address. He also mapped slip numbers to keyword indices, making it possible for him to locate related ideas when needed.[7]

CONTINUES ➤

---

6. Zettelkasten is German for "slip box"—a container for slips of paper.
7. For an excellent overview of Luhmann's system that adapts it to modern technologies, see Sönke Ahrens, *How to Take Smart Notes* (Createspace Independent Publishing Platform, 2017).

CONTINUED ➤

Luhmann's system was decidedly analog, but it shared many characteristics with digital hypertext note-taking systems such as Obsidian and Roam. He viewed his system as a "partner of communication" he'd consult when working on a paper or book. He wrote:

> As a result of extensive work with this technique a kind of secondary memory will arise, an alter ego with who we can constantly communicate. It proves to be similar to our own memory in that it does not have a thoroughly constructed order of its entirety, not hierarchy, and most certainly no linear structure like a book. Just because of this, it gets its own life, independent of its author.[8]

In implementing a knowledge garden along the lines described in this book, you, too, will build an "alter ego" with which to develop ideas. Luhmann noted that such a system takes time to develop. It is only after several years of amassing a database of interconnected thoughts that the system reaches critical mass. So, be patient: your knowledge garden will bear fruit, but it takes some time.

8. Niklas Luhmann, "Communicating with Slip Boxes. An Empirical Account," 1992.

Core Principles for Designing Your Garden

There are lots of different note-taking apps and approaches. Which one you select for your knowledge garden will depend on your particular needs. However, there are a few baseline considerations you should keep in mind when building your system. In particular, your system's components should be *trustworthy*, *open*, and *addressable*. Let's look at these principles in more detail.

Trustworthy Components

Your knowledge garden extends your mind. Your thinking won't flow if you can't trust its components.

Your note repositories should be stable. Things should be where and how you left them when you return. Barring physical damage such as fire or flooding, paper is great in this regard. We still have access to Leonardo's notebooks after five centuries.

Digital note-taking systems aren't as stable. Applications and operating systems come and go, requiring constant upgrades. You must make frequent backups in case things break. Cloud-based apps can be more resilient but require constant internet access. And the organizations that publish them are a potential risk: you can get stuck if the company goes out of business or is acquired.

Your apps should respect your privacy. Ideas may be confidential; you should only share them intentionally. Examine the business models that underwrite system components. Who's paying for it? Is it a commercial application? Open source? Ad-supported? (Avoid ad-supported offerings.)

Easy In, Easy Out

To effectively extend your mind, your knowledge garden must allow you to enter flow states. This won't happen if you're constantly thinking about the mechanics of entering and exporting information into the system. Look for components that make it easy.

Note-taking applications should also make capture fast and easy. You should have as little friction as possible between ideation and capture. This is an area where paper has an edge over digital: you can just open your notebook and start scribbling. But some digital apps are very fast at capture. (The Drafts app on the iPhone excels at speedy capture.)

You can't trust a system that keeps your notes trapped. Look for ways to export your information should you decide to switch. Does the application make exporting easy or hard? Are outgoing notes saved in convenient, widely used formats? Can you export notes in bulk, or do you have to do it one at a time? (This is one of the reasons why I stopped using OneNote.)

WORKING NOTE

Plant an Evergreen Note

Review the inventory of note-taking media you made earlier. Are you capturing any evergreen notes? If so, open that app or notebook and flip through your notes there. Identify one note that draws your attention, perhaps because it contains an important idea or is something you'd like to elaborate. You're going to start an evergreen note in Obsidian for that idea.

Open Obsidian and start a new note. Enter a title that describes the idea succinctly yet clearly. Focus your note on capturing *one* idea rather than several. For example, you may have started a note already to write down what you learn while reading *Duly Noted*. That is too broad. Instead, you may start a note called *Evergreen notes* to capture this one idea from the book. You can revisit this note as you learn more about the concept of evergreen notes over time.

This doesn't mean you can't have a note devoted to *Duly Noted* as a whole. We'll get to that later. For now, simply focus just on capturing individual ideas from the book. You want to clear them out from your existing note capture inboxes and onto Obsidian, which will serve as your trusted repository.

Addressable Notes

Links are foundational to a productive knowledge garden. Your knowledge garden's components should make using links quick and easy. You must be able to navigate easily between related ideas, whether they're on paper—as in Luhmann's zettelkasten—or captured digitally, as in applications like Obsidian and DEVONthink.

At a minimum, every note in your system should have a unique address (whether a web location or a link in your file system) that you can include in other notes. Clicking on that link should take you to the referenced note.[9]

Given that the web is almost three decades old, this should be a given. However, many note-taking apps—including some of the most popular—make quick linking between notes difficult if not outright impossible. Look for note-taking apps that treat intra-note links as first-class citizens.

Endnotes

In this chapter, you've seen tools and steps that comprise a system for thinking. If you develop such a system and use it consistently over time, you'll eventually have a trusted repository of interrelated ideas. While I can't promise you'll be as productive as Niklas Luhmann, you'll have an advantage over people who aren't disciplined about augmenting their minds.

But I must emphasize that achieving critical mass takes discipline and time. For a while, capturing and organizing thoughts will feel like busy work. But this work has value in itself: the fact you're externalizing thoughts will make you more conscientious about how you think. It's practice, and as with everything else, practice will improve your skills.

Over the next four chapters, we'll look at the steps in the process in more detail. We'll start with the critical step of developing the discipline and tools of capturing your thoughts.

---

9. This is a key advantage of building a digital, as opposed to analog, knowledge garden.

5

Don't Let Ideas Get Away

Your attention sucks, and that's a blessing. You wouldn't function if you lingered on everything. Instead, you focus on one thing and then another in quick succession. Useful ideas can get lost among the noise; capturing them gets them out of your head and into the world, where you can refer to them later.

In his 1942 short story *Funes the Memorious*, Jorge Luis Borges tells of a man with an extraordinary memory. After a bad fall, Ireneo Funes awakens to find himself paralyzed yet able to recall everything he's ever experienced: the shapes of clouds on particular days, every crevice in his town, the flowing mane of a horse, and "all the shoots, clusters, and grapes of the vine."[1]

---

1. Jorge Luis Borges, *Ficciones* (New York: Grove Press, 1962).

Sometimes you may wish you had a memory like Funes's. But his "gift" comes with a price. Overloaded with minutiae, he can't think beyond details:

> Without effort, [Funes] had learned English, French, Portuguese, Latin. I suspect, nevertheless, that he was not very capable of thought. To think is to forget a difference, to generalize, to abstract. In the overly replete world of Funes there were nothing but details, almost contiguous details.

While Funes is a fictional character, some people do have extraordinary memories. They, too, remember minute details about their past but struggle when thinking about the present and future. This condition is rare; your memory is likely more ordinary. But you can augment it by scribbling a few words on a sticky note.

Of course, cognition entails more than just remembering. Externalizing thoughts also plays a crucial role in creativity. For example, when writing an essay, making a mind map can give you fresh insights. The map serves as a sort of short-term memory buffer for exploring novel relationships between ideas.

If to think is "to forget a difference, to generalize, to abstract," as Borges claims, your imperfect memory is a blessing: it frees you to jump between levels of abstraction, to analyze the present, to imagine new possibilities. Your ally in these endeavors is the humble note.

But "note" can mean many things. Sometimes, you reach for whatever is close: a sticky note, an old envelope, or the back of your hand. But you can be more intentional about where and how you extend your mind. Your choice of where to capture comes down to what you're trying to do and the context you're doing it in.

Capture Use Cases

Sometimes you have an idea while taking a bath. Sometimes you want to annotate a book. Sometimes you work out the structure for an essay. These cases can all be augmented by capturing thoughts in notes. But how you go at it is different in each case. I consider these to be different means to capture ideas. Let's examine a few common ones.

Capturing on the Run

By "on the run," I don't just mean exercising, but capturing ideas that come to you while you're doing something else. Good ideas can come any time; you must be ready for them. For example, you could be shopping when you think of a perfect opening for your upcoming presentation.

The key is making it easy, so you can quickly return to what you were doing without getting distracted. Pull out your phone, open an app, dictate the idea—done! The challenge is that you might make notes too short or obscure, making them undecipherable later.

Capturing While Listening

Sometimes, you take notes while attending a presentation, lecture, meeting, podcast, or video. As with other notes meant for recall, you want to capture enough to remember the material without getting lost in the weeds. The way around this is to avoid capturing what the speaker says exactly.

When capturing for "gist" (instead of verbatim), it helps to understand the material's structure. Many speakers highlight their main points at the start of their talks: noting those points helps them stay oriented. Another trick is to take notes longhand: many people type faster than they can hand-write, forcing them to listen differently.

How you listen also depends on whether the presentation is live or recorded. Obviously, the latter allows you to pause and skip, making it easier to review unclear points. You can also use AI to transcribe recordings. But while there is a role for transcription, the best lecture notes are those where you synthesize and internalize the material. You can't do it if you're focused on capturing everything exactly.

Capturing While Reading

Taking notes while reading is like having a conversation with the author—your marginal notes riff on their text. It may be a connection with another idea, a reference to another book, a quote that resonates, or something else. Whatever it is, you don't want to lose it.

When reading on paper, scribble in the margins or use small sticky notes and a pencil. The latter also serve as bookmarks to particular ideas. Another approach is using a notebook alongside the book. This gives you more space to sketch diagrams, etc. The downside is that notes are separated from their context. (Suggestion: capture the page number where you found the idea.)

A third approach is taking digital notes on e-books and PDFs. Most e-reading devices and apps let you highlight text and add notes. Depending on which app you use, these notes sync to other devices. Because annotations are digital, you can easily transfer them to other applications later.

Highlighting is an important part of annotating books. You can use different highlighter colors to call out passages that contain key ideas, memorable quotes, open questions, etc. I abide by McPherson's suggestion to highlight no more than 10% of the text and only things you want to remember but don't think you will.[2]

As with so much related to capture, the key to annotating and highlighting what you read is making the notes long enough to be meaningful but short enough not to distract you. Physical margins don't offer enough space to be long-winded, but e-books don't have that constraint. Don't overwhelm yourself.

Capturing While Creating

This modality is different from the others we've discussed. Rather than paying attention to a lecture or book and taking down your thoughts, or capturing ideas on the run, here, you're looking to explore ideas and possibilities. Think of it as "thinking with your hands"—but really, it's your entire body, along with your environment.

For example, I explored many outlines when writing this book. I did much of it using notes in Tinderbox, an app that functions like a whiteboard with digital sticky notes.

Whereas the other note-taking use cases call for capturing quickly so you can get back to what you're doing, generative note-making calls for being expansive. Your focus is on the notes themselves: they're the main attraction. Pick apps and note-taking media that enable flow between you and the "page."

2. Fiona McPherson, *Effective Notetaking* (New Zealand: Wayz Press, 2012).

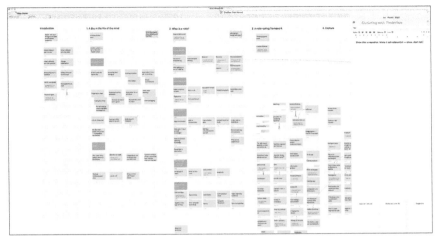

One of the "digital whiteboards" I used while writing *Duly Noted*.

WORKING NOTE
Sync Your Kindle Highlights

Capturing ideas while reading is a common use case for taking notes. If you read e-books, you can sync your notes and highlights with your note's repository. This entails using a paid service called Readwise[3] that imports your highlights and notes from popular reading apps and services such as Kindle, Apple Books, and Kobo. Then you can export them to popular note-taking applications such as Evernote, Notion, Roam, and Obsidian.

CONTINUES ➤

3. https://readwise.io/

CONTINUED ➤

Kindle highlights from the novel *The Glass Bead Game* that have synced to my Obsidian vault via Readwise's connector plug-in. Readwise allows you to define export templates for these synced files.

These notes can include tags. For example, if you come across a passage in a book that includes a memorable quote, you can add a note to the Kindle book that includes the `#quote` hashtag. Tags will come along with the notes automatically. Later, when you're looking for all the notes that include the `#quote` tag, you'll come across that particular Kindle highlight.

Many people resist the lure of e-books. I, too, have a soft spot for paper books. But digital note-taking is compelling, especially for nonfiction. Combined with an aggregator like Readwise, e-books give you a powerful means for collecting knowledge with minimal distractions.[4]

---

4. If you'd prefer an Open Source alternative, some people implement a similar workflow using the Zotero citations manager, which also allows you to annotate PDFs and sync highlights with Obsidian and other note-taking apps.

Media for Capturing Notes

There are as many media available to capture notes as reasons to do so. Knowing the pros and cons of each medium will help you choose one that works best in a given situation.

As mentioned previously, pen and paper have lots of advantages. But they also have limitations that don't apply to digital media. For example, digital information can be organized along many dimensions simultaneously, such as chronologically and by topic. Furthermore, you can store different types of information: text, pictures, audio, etc. Digital is also easier to find and back up.

Still, many people (including me) prefer using analog media for some types of notes. The ideal is to combine the convenience and low friction of analog with the organizational power of digital. I haven't yet found a medium that achieves this fusion perfectly, but you can come close by scanning your paper-based notes. We'll cover how to do this in Chapter 9.

Every Medium Has an Inbox

Think of every note-taking medium as a place to capture a stream of ideas. When you write down ideas in your notebook, you get page after page of notes ordered in the sequence you captured them. The same is true if you take photos, record voice memos, or use your default notes app. These running streams are useful for revisiting recent ideas, but they make it hard to look for older stuff.

It's like continuously piling documents into a physical inbox. Eventually, you'll have to sort through stacks to find what you need. In the next chapter, we'll discuss how to sort your notes into the right places in your system. For now, keep in mind that many note-taking apps have inboxes—and notes in the inbox aren't as useful as those stored where you can find them easily later.

Reduce Friction Using Templates

After you've captured ideas for a while, you'll notice patterns. When you start a new note, you'll think, "This is another one of these." In such cases, templates will speed up your capture time significantly. They'll also remind you of the things you should include when capturing a particular type of idea. Templates reduce friction by allowing you to capture your thoughts quickly without having to think about what to think about.

For example, I keep a "morning notes" journal. That is, every day I write a note that captures a few things about what I'm thinking about, what I learned the previous day, what I plan to accomplish today, etc. I capture these notes in Drafts, which I use as my "catch-all" note-taking app. To ease capture, I've created a simple template that includes the following sections:

- An area for general notes
- What did I learn or improve?
- I'm grateful for: (followed by spaces for three bullet points)
- Goals for today: (followed by spaces for three bullet points)

The title of these journal notes is always the current date, written in the ISO-8601 format we covered in Chapter 2. (Drafts can write the date automatically in this format.) I've assigned a keyboard shortcut for starting one of these daily journal notes, which helps me capture my thoughts without having to think about the format.

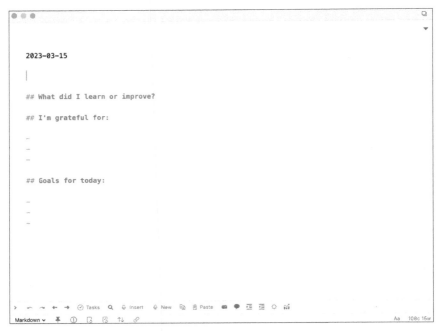

My morning notes template in Drafts. Note that the text is in Markdown. This is because I only use Drafts for capture. I'll save the resulting note to my permanent journal repository in DEVONthink, which uses Markdown natively. There, I can connect the ideas from my morning notes with ideas I've collected elsewhere.

Create a Template

Like many advanced note-taking apps, Obsidian allows you to create templates. To enable this functionality, you must turn on the
Templates plug-in. You do so by opening the application's settings and
going to the *Core* plug-ins section. Once there, you can either search
for the plug-in by name or scroll down the list to the place where the
Templates plug-in is listed. There you can toggle it on.

Templates is one of the core plug-ins that ships with Obsidian. Core plug-
ins must be turned on for their functionality to become available.

Notice that the Templates plug-in listing has a gear icon next to its toggle. Clicking on this icon reveals the plug-in's configuration panel. There,
you can adjust details of how the plug-in works. The most important
configuration is the folder where you want to save templates.

CONTINUES ➤

The Templates plug-in configuration panel. The first field asks for a folder location for templates. Notice mine starts with an underscore: this is a hack that makes this folder appear before normally named files when sorted alphabetically.

Obsidian will treat files saved in this location as templates. To apply a template, go to a note and click on the "Insert template" button on the toolbar along the left side of the window. This will insert the content of the template into that note. (If the note isn't empty, it won't erase its contents—but you may have to copy and paste stuff to place it into the right locations.)

The "Insert template" button in Obsidian's toolbar.

Like regular notes, you write templates in Markdown. However, Obsidian provides some special codes to insert variables like the file name and date automatically. This is the Markdown code for the template I use when capturing notes of books and papers I've read:

```
---
created: {{date}} {{time}}
url:
---

## {{title}}

### Meta

Title:: {{title}}
Author::
Publisher::
Year::
DOI::

### Notes

### Criticism and influence

### References

- [[{{title}} (highlights)]]
- Bookends
- Amazon

#litnotes
```

CONTINUES ➤

CONTINUED ➤

The items wrapped in curly brackets are variables that Obsidian will insert by default whenever I apply this template to a note. So, if I start a blank note named *The Glass Bead Game* and apply this template to the note, Obsidian will replace all instances of {{title}} with the words *The Glass Bead Game*.

The references section in this template is where I add links to other notes in my vault and to external references such as Bookends (a citation management app) and the book's Amazon page. Notice the first item under references: it's a wikilink to another note in my vault that has the note's title followed by the word *highlights* in parentheses. When I apply this template to a note called *The Glass Bead Game*, Obsidian will render the line thus:

```
- [[The Glass Bead Game (highlights)]]
```

As you saw earlier in the chapter, I use Readwise to sync my Kindle annotations. I've configured Readwise to append the word *highlights* in parentheses to the names of notes it creates from these annotations. After I annotate the e-book, a note named *The Glass Bead Game (highlights)* will automatically appear in my vault. So, as long as my new note's title matches the name of the book in Readwise, this template will automatically link my new note to the one containing this e-book's highlights.

Some Final Tips

While it might seem that capturing notes is the most basic part of the process, it's possible to do it more effectively. Keeping these tips in mind will improve your ability to extend your mind with notes while remaining present.

Be Primed to Capture

The key to effective capture is doing as little of it as feasible, so you can return to whatever you were doing as quickly as possible. "As feasible" means capturing enough, so you can get back to the thought later and have it make sense. So, you must balance capturing too much and too little—and do it quickly. This process calls for optimizing capture to allow you to take down ideas the moment they emerge.

Photographers aspire to capture "the decisive moment": an exact action or situation that makes for a special picture. In pursuit of this goal, they value cameras that allow them to snap a shot quickly. Photographer Chase Jarvis said that "the best camera is the one you have with you." A fancy tool with many features won't help you if it's at home; better to have a simpler tool that's with you when the opportunity presents itself.

In the same spirit, you should always have means to capture your thoughts. It doesn't have to be a notebook; your phone is a powerful note-taking device. You could use the built-in Notes app, email yourself, dictate a voice recording, snap a photograph, and more. Powerful devices and small paper notebooks are relatively cheap and widely available. Use them.

Capture Just Enough

As you saw in Chapter 4, effective capture requires being present. And yet, writing down a thought—whether on paper or digitally—takes you out of the moment: you stop paying attention to the situation or person for a moment. By the time you're back, you may have missed a beat.

You want to return to the situation as quickly as possible. This calls for capturing short notes—just a few words or a quick sketch. And yet, how many times have you picked up a short note you wrote a while back to realize you have no idea what it refers to?

For example, imagine you're out for a walk and see a poster advertising a concert you'd like to attend three weeks from now. You open your notes app and write "9/27 8 pm" to remind you. When you revisit the note a week later, you stare at it in befuddlement, struggling to recall what it's about.

How little is too little and how much is too much? The answer is different for different people; some have better memories than others, so a few words might suffice. My memory isn't good, so I err on the side of capturing more context than I think I need. I'm grateful weeks later when I revisit my note and pick up the thread without missing a beat.

Be Mindful of What You're Paying Attention To

McPherson argues that the most important skill in studying might be distinguishing between important and unimportant information.[5] The principle applies universally to all forms of note-taking: you want to focus on what matters.

For example, if you're listening to a history lecture, what the speaker says matters more than what he or she is wearing: focus on the message, not the messenger. Moreover, given its subject, you can listen for key events, people, institutions, and technologies that influenced the story.

You'd listen for different things if it was instead a lecture about chemistry or a team progress meeting. Knowing what you're paying attention to helps you hone your attention, so you don't waste time capturing things that don't matter.

Know Whether You're Capturing for Keeps

We've already covered the distinction between evergreen and transient notes. Knowing which you're capturing changes how you capture. Transient notes can be looser and more minimal, whereas permanent notes require more attention and care.

For example, the concert reminder is only useful before the event. Conversely, you may be reading a book for work and learn about an idea that resonates with you. You want to capture it to revisit it later and connect it with other relevant ideas. This note has a longer lifespan, so you may want to capture more context, so it makes sense when you return to it in the future.

Also, consider whether you're note-taking or note-making. In both cases, putting pen to paper (or typing into a computer) changes how you pay attention, allowing you to filter out distractions. If you pay better attention by doodling on your notebook, your notes might not reflect what you heard— but if it helps you think better, then it's a valid reason for taking notes.

5. Fiona McPherson, *Effective Notetaking* (New Zealand: Wayz Press, 2012).

NOTABLE NOTE-TAKER
Nicole van der Hoeven

Nicole van der Hoeven is a Developer Advocate at Grafana Labs, a company that builds software development tools. She likes to "learn in public" by sharing via her blog, digital garden, and YouTube, where she hosts a channel focused on teaching how to use Obsidian. She writes,

> I consider myself a knowledge worker: a significant part of my job depends on how quickly I learn new technologies and how clearly I can impart what I've learned to others…Remaining relevant in tech pretty much requires that you learn a lot, learn quickly, and enjoy the hell out of it. Luckily, Obsidian is pretty great at this.[6]

I interviewed Nicole to learn more about one of her use cases for notes: playing and managing tabletop role-playing games, or RPGs. These games are created by their participants, who role-play as characters having adventures they devise using their imaginations. One player (the "dungeon master") leads the story and sets forth challenges for the party.

Games span several days or even weeks, and the dungeon master must maintain continuity. It helps to have an "extensible knowledge base," which is how Nicole describes Obsidian. Individual notes can describe different locations in the world, and those notes can be linked to other notes to create a record of the party's interactions in the world.

CONTINUES ➤

6. https://nicolevanderhoeven.com/blog/20210518-how-i-use-obsidian-at-work/

CONTINUED ➤

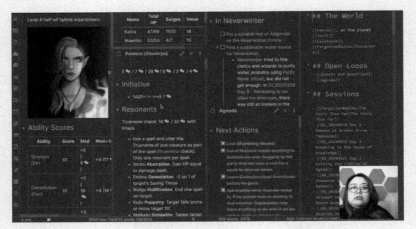

A still from a YouTube video where Nicole describes how she uses Obsidian for RPGs, both as a player and dungeon master.[7]

People played tabletop role-playing games before personal computers were available. Early players tracked their adventures using paper. But connected note-taking tools take the experience to another level. Knowledge gardens aren't just for learning and working: they can also be playgrounds.

7. www.youtube.com/watch?v=3pt6_srUZ7U&t=188s

Endnotes

David Allen, author of the classic productivity book *Getting Things Done (GTD)*, advocates cultivating a "mind like water": a clear mental state that's open to new information. This entails capturing commitments in a trusted system so the mind can focus on other things.[8]

While GTD focuses on commitments, the same applies to other thoughts. "Fixing" ideas in the world releases you from keeping everything in your head. Knowing that your thinking is externalized somewhere safe and stable gives you a sense of looseness and flexibility. And, of course, cognition isn't just about memory: capturing ideas allows you to develop and explore relationships between them.

Effective capture requires finding a sweet spot between taking down too little and too much. Capturing just-enough context becomes natural over time—but it takes practice. But capturing an idea doesn't guarantee you'll find it later. That requires planning, a reasonable system for long-term storage, and the discipline to use it.

8. David Allen, *Getting Things Done: The Art of Stress-Free Productivity* (New York: Penguin, 2015).

6

Put Everything in Its Right Place

Capturing ideas isn't enough. For your garden to help you think better, you must also find and use stuff. Whereas capture aims for presence of mind and flow, long-term storage makes it easier for "future you" to find relevant ideas without overwhelming "present you."

It's a perennial struggle. In *The History of Navigation* (1704), John Locke advised travelers to carefully observe the places they visit and not let observations be influenced by others' writings,

> for upon comparing their observations with other mens, they will often find a very considerable difference. Let them therefore always have a table-book at hand to set down every thing worth remembering, and then at night more methodically transcribe the notes they have taken in the day.[1]

---

1. John Locke, *The Works of John Locke: In Nine Volumes* (9) (1824).

Inspired by accounting methods, early modern scholars, such as Locke, kept different types of notebooks. They used "waste books" to temporarily store ideas, some of which they'd transfer later into more structured "commonplace books."[2] Locke himself devised a method for indexing ideas to make them easier to find.[3]

There are many such methods you can use to find your stuff. We've already discussed how to link notes into emergent structures that organize information from the bottom-up. In this chapter, we'll discuss how to organize notes from the top-down so you can find and use them later.

From Need to Information (and Back Again)

Many people feel overwhelmed by information. But there are approaches for coping. One that's worth looking into is *personal information management* (PIM), which focuses on helping individuals organize their stuff.

In *Keeping Found Things Found*, William Jones writes, "PIM activities are an effort to establish, use, and maintain a mapping between information and need."[4] This notion of "mapping" a need and information is important for understanding how to best organize notes. Let's unpack these terms.

Imagine you're planning to cook an elaborate dish and discover you're missing key ingredients. Before going to the store, you write down what you need. This list makes shopping fast and easy. But without it, you may find yourself standing among the aisles struggling to remember what you needed to buy.

In this scenario, the *need* is getting the necessary ingredients. Completing that task serves a higher-level need: preparing a particular dish. And completing *that* task might be in service to an even higher-level need. For example, you might be celebrating a milestone with the dinner.

The list of ingredients is *information*: it reminds you what you need when you can do something about it (i.e., at the store). By the way, if you stash the list in a pocket, you must remember which pocket it's in. The information's location is also information: the list won't be of much use if you can't find it when needed.

2. Ann M. Blair, *Too Much to Know: Managing Scholarly Information Before the Modern Age* (New Haven: Yale University Press, 2011).
3. https://jillianhess.substack.com/p/john-lockes-pursuit-of-the-perfect
4. William Jones, *Keeping Found Things Found: The Study and Practice of Personal Information Management* (Burlington: Morgan Kaufmann, 2010).

A *mapping* connects you with the correct information at the right time. Some mappings are external to you, such as the note with the ingredients. But other mappings are *internal*: they don't have tangible representations. For example, always keeping shopping lists in your left back pocket is an internal mapping: if you stick to the habit, you won't have to ever think about it again.

This example seems trivial because you're unlikely to forget the note is in your pocket if you just stashed it there twenty minutes ago. But much information has a longer shelf life: you might need it next week or five years from now. So, it's important to know where to find pointers to where stuff is. (This is why indexes are always in the back of books: that's where we expect them.)

So far, we've discussed mapping information to needs. But the relationship also goes the other way: information spurs needs. This is obvious in advertising, which aims to implant desires in your mind. But it's also the case with notes. You've experienced this if you've ever brainstormed by outlining: adding an item to the outline brings to mind other items that should be there.

You can tell that a mapping of information to a need works when you can easily find stuff when you need it. But most often, you only notice when you can't—and it's especially frustrating when it's something you wrote. AI can help but creating good mapping will get you a long way. You can do it through mindful use of containers and metadata.

Storing Stuff in Containers

When you consider organizing stuff, you may think of defining containers to hold your stuff: file folders, computer directories, library shelves, etc. In your knowledge garden, you put notes into groups where you expect to find them later. There are two basic approaches for doing this: piling and filing.

Piling

Piling is just as it sounds: lumping stuff in a pile. Before computers, people did this on (physical) desktops: new bills went into an "inbox" tray or "incoming" pile. Once in a while, people would go through these items and transcribe them, file them, or toss them.

You may have several such piles on your desk. They're convenient, since they keep stuff "at hand." But they don't scale; you'll lose track of stuff if you have many piles. (Physical) piles make finding older things difficult.

Of course, computers also have piles. You likely stash documents, pictures, scans, and other stuff in clusters on your computer's desktop. As mentioned previously, most note-taking apps also have a special container that behaves like an endless pile: the inbox.[5]

You may use various apps to capture notes. This creates an additional burden, since you must then triage many inboxes. Aim for as few inboxes as feasible. Avoid using apps that provide similar features and functionality. Use automation to consolidate notes into as few piles as possible.[6]

There are limits with how much paper you can manage before getting buried. Computers don't have those constraints: you can keep adding stuff and use search to bail you out. But piling isn't a long-term strategy; if you don't organize your inboxes periodically, you'll get an unusable mess. And the messier it becomes, the harder it is to organize, resulting in a vicious cycle.

Filing

Filing involves storing notes in containers where you can find them later. This process entails defining categories that make sense to "future you"— challenging, since you'll have different needs and interests in the future. By "formal," I mean sets based on predefined categories. Think of labeled hanging folders: you may have one for insurance, another for taxes, etc. These are analogs of the folders and directories in your computer.[7]

Unlike physical folders, digital containers can contain unlimited containers and sub-containers. That is, you can save folders inside folders inside folders. Digital containers can only have one "parent" container at a time: a folder can contain several sub-folders but can't be contained in more than one folder. The same applies for containers in many note-taking apps.[8]

---

5. Some apps, such as OneNote, let you specify a particular container as the inbox. Others, such as Notability, provide a dedicated container called *Unfiled Notes* for this purpose.
6. This is feasible if your operating system and apps allow for interoperability. For example, I use Notability to take notes by hand on my iPad. Notability saves notes in its own inbox by default, but I don't organize them there. Instead, I've configured the app to save PDF backups to a Dropbox folder. These PDFs are copied nightly to my DEVONthink inbox, where I sort them later into the proper files.
7. This is no accident: early computer designers intentionally chose the file/folder metaphor because it maps to our real-world experience of managing information.
8. That said, some operating systems and applications support the concept of file *aliases*: pointers to a file that looks like the file and which can be placed in different containers.

Common Categorization Frameworks

Imagine you're working on several projects that require you to take meeting minutes. After a while, you'll have lots of such notes. How do you group them, so you can find them later? There are several approaches you can take. You could do it by date (i.e., chronologically), by the people involved, or by project. While there are seemingly endless possibilities, there are two taxonomies worth examining: LATCH and PARA.

LATCH

Information architect Richard Saul Wurman suggests there are five ways of organizing information, which he summarizes with the acronym LATCH:[9]

- **Location,** for items related to a particular locale—whether it be a city, country, body part, etc.

- **Alphabet,** which is useful for large collections of homogeneous information.

- **Time,** for items that are related to a particular moment, such as a journal or diary.

- **Category,** which is useful for organizing diverse items that are otherwise related somehow. Think of the aisles in a supermarket.

- **Hierarchy,** which groups things based on their magnitude or relative importance, such as price ranges or size differences.

LATCH isn't definitive; some people have suggested variations. Moreover, the category and hierarchy groupings are very broad. Still, this can be a good starting point for your groupings.

CONTINUES ➤

---

9. Richard Saul Wurman, *Information Anxiety 2* (Carmel, IN: Que Publishing, 2001).

CONTINUED ➤

Many note-taking apps let you sort items alphabetically or chronologically. So really, the main dimensions to consider are location, category, and hierarchy. Whichever you choose, be consistent: if you use time as your primary taxonomy, don't mix in folders organized by category or hierarchy.

PARA

LATCH's "category" grouping is very broad. After all, anything can be a category. How do you decide how to categorize your notes?

One approach is to group them by the type of content they represent: meeting minutes, book notes, web bookmarks, etc. Another approach is to group notes by the context they serve: some are related to projects, while others are long-term reference materials.

An example of this approach is Tiago Forte's PARA, which proposes a four-group classification:[10]

- **Projects,** which have a deadline
- **Areas,** which are ongoing
- **Resources,** for material that doesn't belong in either an area or project
- **Archives,** for storage of inactive projects, areas, or resources

Why keep stuff that's no longer active? Because computers have lots of space and excellent search capabilities. You might need to revisit old materials at some point, so you don't lose much by keeping them. That said, you don't want them distracting you during day-to-day work.

---

10. Tiago Forte, *Building a Second Brain: A Proven Method to Organize Your Digital Life and Unlock Your Creative Potential* (New York: Simon and Schuster, 2022).

Which is to say, filing requires more forethought than piling. Things in containers should be related—i.e., they should cover the same subject or topic. You must think up front about those categories. For example, bank statements might go under *financial documents* and recipes under *wellness*. Creating a good taxonomy can be challenging if you have many types of things. Moreover, the taxonomy will change over time.

Suggestions for Sensible Filing

As with many things in personal knowledge management (PKM), it's possible to go overboard with containers. You can easily end up with lots of folders with slightly different names, which will make your job more difficult. The following suggestions will help you implement a sensible container strategy.

Name Containers for Clarity

Since containers store notes for the long-term, clear names matter. You should be able to scan your list of folders and quickly locate the one you're looking for. This calls for consistent patterns that highlight key distinctions between containers.

Avoid ambiguous labels. For example, the labels *Project 1*, *Project 2*, and *Project 3* might be short, but in a few years, you might not remember what *Project 2* referred to. A clearer name would be something like *Alaska vacation*—or *Alaska vacation 2016* for future variations of that project.

Because many apps let you sort containers alphabetically, the first few characters are important. *Alaska vacation 2016* will appear before *Bahamas vacation 2018*. Consider which distinction might matter more to future you: the destination (*Alaska, Bahamas*), the year, or the fact that it's a vacation. If it's the latter, name your folders *Vacation Alaska 2016* and *Vacation Bahamas 2018* instead, which will keep vacations together when sorted alphabetically.

Aim for Just Enough Containers

Computers don't have practical limits on how many containers you can create, so you may be tempted to create a folder for every grouping that comes to mind. That's a mistake. The more folders you have, the harder it is to find what you're looking for. And when you're organizing your notes, it's harder to decide where each should go. Large collections are also harder to maintain.

Follow the "seven plus or minus two" rule: aim for between five and nine sub-folders in any given container.[11] If you see more than nine documents or notes in a container, you might need a new container. The result is a hierarchy that has depth and breadth rather than one that's flat, with lots of peer sub-folders.

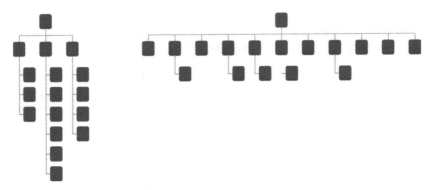

Deep versus broad hierarchical structures.

An exception is containers meant as long-term archives of inactive or infrequently used materials. In this case, you aren't concerned with how many sub-folders you have, since you won't use them day-to-day. But do name your folders clearly so that you can locate them when you need them.

Save Stuff Where "Future You" Will Find It

Some notes obviously go in specific containers. If you're writing about a vacation to Alaska, the *Alaska vacation* folder is the obvious container. But some things aren't easy to categorize up front. It may be that a note straddles two or more categories. Where should it go?

It sounds easy to say, "put it where you'll find it later." But how do you do that? Where will "future you" be likely to look for this thing? It's not an easy decision; what makes logical sense to you now might not make sense in a month.

I've learned to go with my gut. Whenever I wonder, "where should I store this?" some place pops to mind. Occasionally, it's a location that doesn't make logical sense but *feels* right. My sense is that if this is where I think it

11. G. A. Miller, "The Magical Number Seven, Plus or Minus Two: Some Limits on Our Capacity for Processing Information," *Psychological Review*, 63, no. 2 (1956): 81–97.

should go now, "future me" will assume the same. This approach hasn't failed me yet. Conversely, whenever I overthink storage by creating elaborate top-down organization schemes, I misplace things.

Kevin Kelly offers useful advice on how to decide where things should be stored:

> If you are looking for something in your house and you finally find it, when you are done with it, don't put it back where you found it. Put it back where you first looked for it.[12]

How you organize your personal notes doesn't need to make sense to anyone else.[13] "Go with what feels right" applies as much to your notes as it does to other stuff, and the stakes are lower since you can use search. And, of course, you can move things later if needed.

Use Dedicated Applications for Particular Information Types

LATCH and PARA can be used to organize different types of information: meeting minutes, documentation, general notes, etc. Some of these types have particular structures and uses that are best managed in specialized applications.

Events—concepts tied to a specific date and time—belong in your calendar. Contact details go into contact management and CRM apps. Commitments should be in to-do apps. There are also specialized applications for managing bookmarks and literature references.

Storing stuff in specialized applications has two advantages. First, these apps are structured to make storing and finding these particular types of information faster. Second, keeping stuff in particular applications relieves you from wondering where they might be when you need them.

Of course, it helps that applications can interoperate. For example, many macOS applications provide a Share menu that lets them send items to other apps. You should favor apps that are good citizens of their OS ecosystem. (Alas, this is one of Obsidian's shortcomings: since it's designed as a cross-platform app, it doesn't use some OS-specific capabilities.)

---

12. Kevin Kelly, *Excellent Advice for Living: Wisdom I Wish I'd Known Earlier* (New York: Viking, 2023).
13. This principle is obviously moot if you're in a collaborative situation. More on that in Chapter 10.

Metadata

Containers aren't the only way to organize your stuff. You can also define attributes that describe notes so you can find them later. Common strategies include clear, consistent naming and using metadata such as tags. We discussed naming in Chapter 2, so let's focus on metadata.

Metadata is an abstract idea, but one that's important to understand if you want to organize your notes effectively. The gist: *metadata is data that provides information about other data.* See, I told you it's abstract. Let's dig into it with an example.

Imagine that you're hiking in Northern California. You see a spectacular view, so you take a photograph with your phone. Years later, a friend says they're planning to visit the region, so you tell them about the hike. "Here," you say, "let me show you a picture." You open your photos app, go to its map, and look for the photos you took at that location.

Apple Photos uses metadata to help you find your pictures. The application enables you to change some of this metadata, such as the date and time when you took the photo.

Clear Your Inboxes

Return to the note-taking media inventory you wrote down in Chapter 4. Rows represent several piles you've captured. Some, you'll want to keep for later.

MEDIUM	PURPOSE	EVERGREEN?
Stickies	Reminders	No
Notes app	Shopping lists	No
Notes app	Books to read	Yes
Paper slips	Shopping lists	No

As you revisit your inboxes, you'll see different types of notes: some will have contact details for other people, some will have reminders, and some will be notes about meetings. Move contact details, events, and commitments to dedicated apps such as contact managers, calendars, and to-do managers.

Some notes, such as meeting minutes for a project, won't fit in any one of these specialized apps. Consider starting a container in your computer (or your notes app) for that project. (Alternatively, you may start a folder to collect all meeting minutes.)

Your phone captures more than just pixels when it takes a photo. In addition to the pixels that make up the image, the phone captures data that *describes* the photo: its location, the date and time, the aperture, etc. The picture is the *data*, and all this other stuff—time, location, camera settings—is *metadata*.

When you show your friend, the picture is what you want them to see; metadata are there to help you find the picture among the many thousands in your photo collection. Some metadata, such as file creation and modification dates, are set automatically. Many applications also allow you to add and edit metadata such as descriptions, tags, ratings, and more.

Tagging

Tags are a type of metadata you add to items to describe them. You can tag physical notes,[14] but paper-based tagging systems are cumbersome. Computers change that because tagging digital stuff is easy. In many Markdown-based apps, all you need to do is add the hash (#) character before a word to turn it into a tag.

One way to understand the advantages of tags is to contrast them with filing containers. As I noted earlier, often each note lives in one "parent" container at a time. Tagging is different: you can add multiple tags to a note or document to create "matrixed" groupings. For example, you could organize a note by both project *and* type simultaneously.

Whereas containers separate notes into discrete groups, tags do the opposite: they associate notes. For example, you may want to see all the notes you wrote in December 2021, regardless of where they're stored. Because date and time are metadata associated with notes, you can see all the notes you captured in a particular month.

Many note-taking apps allow you to assign tags to notes and then see lists of all notes that have those tags. For example, you could add a tag called #ToDo and then see a list of all notes assigned that tag. They may be in different folders, but the tag brings them together in one view. After you complete each task, you can remove the tag from its note, which removes it from the list.

You can add as many tags as you want. Each time you do, the note becomes part of the set of notes that also have that tag and subsets that include that tag and others.

COMMON CHALLENGES WITH TAGS

While tags are convenient, they also have downsides. It's easy to go overboard. Having too many tags creates friction, since you must think about which tag to add. You can end up managing slight variations of the same term. For example, you might use the #book tag to describe one book and #books on another.

---

14. Locke's approach to indexing his notes looks a lot like modern tagging.

But it might be even worse: #book and #books might *not* refer to the same thing, so you must remember the difference between them. It can also be hard to use tags consistently. Typos can lead to a proliferation of unintended variations. (Fortunately, many apps autocomplete tags.)

Another challenge is dealing with multiple apps that use tags but don't sync with each other. This results in managing parallel sets of tags, which is becoming more of an issue as PKM apps proliferate. There are no adequate solutions to these issues for now, apart from being mindful about tag use.

HOW TO USE TAGS EFFECTIVELY

Using tags effectively requires discipline and mindfulness—but it's worth it. Here are a few pointers that will help you use tags more effectively:

- **Less is more.** As a rule of thumb, stick to between one and three tags per item; more than that, and you'll spend inordinate amounts of time tagging things.

- **Decide how you'll use tags.** Will they describe what the item is about? What project it belongs to? Who created it? Etc.

- **Decide on grammatical rules.** For example, will you tag an item representing a book as #books, since it belongs to the "books" group, or #book, since it describes a single book?

- **Decide on a text format.** All lowercase? camelCase? CapitalCamelCase? flatcase? snake_case? kebab-case? Etc. (This choice might not be entirely up to you; some apps prefer some types over others.)

Here are a few ways to use tags:

- As **semantic descriptors**, for describing what something *is*. E.g., #book = "this item represents a book."

- As **grouping descriptors**, for associating items with other related items. E.g., #dulynoted = "this item is related to the book I'm writing."

- As **state indicators**, for setting up workflows. E.g., #unread = "you haven't gotten to this one yet."

- As **action flags**, which are also useful for workflows. E.g., #todo = "this is an item you must act on somehow."

Of course, you can mix schemes and use search, smart folders, or groups to build punch lists, track books you'd like to read, organize projects, etc.

Tag Your Notes

Some apps, such as Apple Notes, provide special fields for tags. Others, such as Obsidian, let you type tags directly as part of the note's text. You do this by adding a hash character (#) to the beginning of any word. For example, if you want to tag a note as being about a meeting, you can type the word #meeting anywhere in its body.

Obsidian considers any string of alphanumeric characters after the hash and before the next punctuation to be the tag's label. Tags can't include spaces. There are several ways to deal with this issue. One is to run the words together (e.g., #meetingminutes). You could also capitalize the first letter of each word (#MeetingMinutes) to make it more legible.

If you use tags consistently, you'll eventually have a rich set of connections between notes. However, you'll also have lots of free-form text snippets in dozens or hundreds of notes, which can make changes harder. What happens if you want to change the spelling of a tag or consolidate two tags into one? In Chapter 9, I'll show you a third-party plug-in that makes managing tags easier.

For example, I commonly tag some bookmarks as both #book (a semantic description of what the thing is) and #wishlist (which describes *why* I'm keeping it). A search for bookmarks with both tags generates my book wishlist. If I buy a book later, I either remove the #wishlist tag or delete the bookmark.

This is powerful stuff. But as I mentioned previously, don't go overboard. Avoid more than three or so tags per item. Keep group, workflow, and state indicators simple. And be consistent; this isn't an area where you want to continually innovate.

Other Tips and Recommendations

Throughout this chapter, we've covered suggestions for organizing your notes using both containers and metadata. Here are some final recommendations that will help in either case.

Batch Organizing Tasks

It's easier to keep your system organized if you do it regularly. How often you do it will depend on how quickly stuff accrues. For example, I clear out my email inbox daily and my DEVONthink inbox around once per week. The latter takes about an hour to do, but it saves me time when I must look for stuff later.

Archive During Capture

It will be easier to organize your inboxes if they don't have too many notes to begin with. One way to achieve this is by archiving notes immediately when you capture them. It's not always feasible, since you may be in a rush. But if you know exactly what you're capturing, you can add tags and save the note to the right folder during capture.

Increase the Contrast in Distinctions

When creating folders or tags, you'll sometimes come across ambiguous names. To clarify them, you must amplify the distinctions between them. For example, the word "study" can be both a noun and a verb. If you use the label in a tag or a folder name, you might be confused about what it means later. In those cases, consider either finding a different word (e.g., "report") or appending a clarifying word (e.g., "marketing study").

Don't Overstructure Things

The more elaborate your organizational structures (i.e., folders and tags), the more choices you'll have when deciding how to organize your notes, which adds cognitive friction. Keep things simple and minimal: aim for a small set of tags that describe things practically rather than theoretically. The objective isn't to create a beautiful taxonomy, but to think better.

NOTABLE NOTE-TAKER

Kourosh Dini

Kourosh Dini is a psychiatrist and psychoanalyst, author, and productivity expert, and author of the book *Taking Smart Notes with DEVONthink*. In an interview on my podcast, Kourosh offered a practical approach for using tags.[15] Specifically, he suggested avoiding "associational tagging"—i.e., adding everything that comes to mind about the note in an effort to describe it.

Instead of associational tagging, Kourosh suggests having a clear purpose for each tag. For example, while researching the psychodynamics of ADHD, he collected over 300 notes. He tagged them as relevant to that project. Later, he could see all the notes he'd tagged and export them to Scrivener as fodder for the writing process.

In the past, I've fallen into the trap of writing a note and trying to think of all the ways I could describe what it's about. For example, if it's an idea I've read in a book about content strategy, I might add the tags #uxdesign, #content, #contentstrategy, #publication, etc.

This approach adds friction. Thinking about all the ways to tag the note takes time and effort. It's also hard to be consistent: I may add certain tags to an idea one day and use a different set for a similar idea the following week. As a result, many people avoid tagging altogether—a wasted opportunity.

After speaking with Kourosh, I became more intentional and minimal when tagging. Rather than trying to cover all possible angles, I now tag most notes with a project or theme. For example, I have a collection of notes tagged #dulynoted. I haven't bothered with other descriptors; what matters is that they inform this book's writing.

15. http://theinformed.life/2021/01/31/episode-54-kourosh-dini/

Don't Let Folders or Tags Proliferate

Sometimes, you'll make a note that doesn't fit anywhere. You'll be tempted to create a new folder or tag on the spot. Resist this temptation. Think instead if there might be a broader container that might hold it. It's okay to have a folder labeled "other" and to leave items untagged; your computer's search capabilities can often help you find outliers. Again, be practical.

Endnotes

As you've seen, the goal of organizing your notes is finding the stuff you need at the right time. You organize notes by filing, piling, or tagging them. Files are for storage, piles are for processing, and metadata let you connect items stored in different locations.

While piles and files are mutually exclusive (you pile things while working and file them when you're done), tagging can apply to either. Knowing when to use them will make it easier for you to look for stuff in the future. As my friend Karl Fast puts it (I'm paraphrasing), "Folders are for dividing and tags are for joining."

Bottom line: use containers such as folders and groups to get things out of inboxes and into more permanent places where you can find them later. Use tags to connect stuff that belongs to the same set but not necessarily in the same container.

So far, we've covered organizational approaches that John Locke and his contemporaries might have recognized—even though they'd be blown away by our technologies. In the next chapter, we'll see how computers take the organization of thoughts and ideas to another level.

7

Spark Insights

Capturing, linking, and organizing notes systematically takes work. What's the point? The point is twofold: becoming more adept at managing the onslaught of information and thinking better. You already know notes can augment your memory. Now, let's turn to how notes can help you have better ideas. Specifically, let's look at how mindful organization of information can spark insights.

Consider the periodic table. You likely learned about it in school: a matrix of the known chemical elements such as gold, aluminum, hydrogen, and silicon—the stuff that stuff is made from. As a child, I thought the table was something that had always been there. But it's a designed thing—and relatively recently. It took centuries for people to recognize the elements we know today.

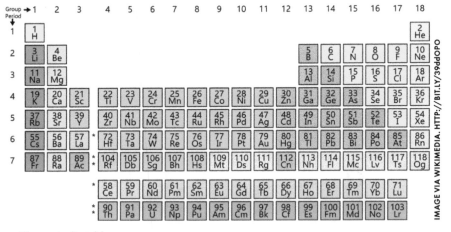

The periodic table.

The periodic table is the work of 19th century chemist Dmitri Mendeleev. Mendeleev and his colleagues noticed patterns—relationships—in how elements interact with each other. The table manifests those patterns, which are inherent in nature. It's organized in columns, which represent groups, and rows, which represent periods. Elements in groups and periods share characteristics.

Which is to say, the periodic table emerged from an insight: the fact that elements have some characteristics in common, and those characteristics repeat periodically. Arranging elements into a structure that reflected those patterns revealed a further insight: that some elements were "missing"—i.e., the structure called for them to be there, but they hadn't yet been identified.

The periodic table is an example of how thinking about information systematically can lead to organizing it differently, leading to insights. And having more and better insights is one of the ultimate goals of building a knowledge garden.

What Are Insights?

Think back to a time when you had an "a-ha!" moment: you suddenly understood a difficult concept, solved a puzzle, or had a creative breakthrough. Perhaps remembering the occasion makes you feel good. But you may also feel a bit frustrated at the realization that *you don't know exactly how you did it.*

Insights are like sneezes: you can't force them. You may have read stories—or had the experience yourself—of struggling to solve a problem, only to wake up to the obvious solution after (literally) sleeping on it. Or an answer might pop in your mind while showering or taking a walk. Sometimes it feels as though anything works other than focusing on the problem at hand.

So, if you can't force insights, how can your note-taking system spur them? To explore this, we must look more closely at what insights *are*. In *Seeing What Others Don't*, Gary Klein provides a working definition of insight: "an unexpected shift to a better story."[1] Klein is referring to causal stories: how we explain to ourselves how things happened or may happen; the cause-effect relationships between concepts.

You solve the puzzle by gaining a new understanding of the relationships between elements. You experience a creative breakthrough after reframing a problem. You understand the concept after finding an analogy that allows you to integrate it into your existing knowledge. Yes, I'm talking again about *models*.

Models

Models are ideas about how things might be organized and how they might work.[2] For example, consider the idea that the Earth orbits the Sun. Like the periodic table, you likely learned this at an early age and have taken it for granted since. You haven't directly observed this phenomenon but have experienced its effects, such as the changing positions of stars in the night sky.

Still, you have ideas about how this works. These ideas include distinctions (e.g., the Earth and the Sun are different bodies, with different masses, compositions, and characteristics) and relationships (e.g., these bodies relate in particular ways through the force of gravity). You can imagine a diagram with little circles drawing elliptical paths around each other. That's a model.

You experience an insight when one of your models shifts. It might be that you've become aware of new information that allows you to relate two other concepts in a new way. Or perhaps it changes your understanding of how existing elements relate to each other. Whatever the case, an unexpected and sudden shift happens in your understanding of how things are organized and how they work.

---

1. Gary Klein, *Seeing What Others Don't: The Remarkable Ways We Gain Insights* (New York: PublicAffairs Books, 2013).
2. Hugh Dubberly, "Models of Models," *Interactions* 16, no. 3 (2009): 54–60.

Mind Maps

Mind Maps®, which were originated by Tony Buzan in the early 1970s, are a visual way of exploring the distinctions and relationships between the concepts that define a particular domain. It's like a two-dimensional outline where you dump onto a page what you know about the subject: how it's organized, its main components, their names, etc.

To draw a mind map, start with a large blank sheet of paper. In the center, write down the main idea you want to explore. This idea is the central node in your diagram. You then draw branches radiating from that central node to the subject's main sub-categories. These sub-nodes, too, can have sub-nodes, leading to a rich network of relationships between ideas.

For example, if you were mind-mapping this book, you'd write *Duly Noted* in the center of the page. Then think about the main areas you'd like to explore about the book: it could be note-taking tools, practices, principles, and so on. These will become branches radiating out from the words *Duly Noted*.

So, write the words *Tools*, *Practices*, and *Principles* around the node labeled *Duly Noted* and draw lines to connect them to that central node. You then repeat the process for each sub-branch. For example, think about the tools you've learned about so far in the book and write them around the node labeled *Tools*. These will become branches of the *Tools* node in the same way that *Tools* is a branch of *Duly Noted*. You can do the same for the other sub-branches.

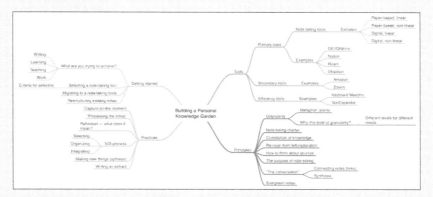

A mind map for a workshop that eventually led to this book.

It's easy to draw mind maps using pen and paper or sticky notes on a whiteboard. But there are also mind-mapping apps, such as Xmind and MindNode. The "infinite canvas" app Miro also includes mind-mapping features. While paper may be faster for getting ideas down, one advantage of these apps is that they let you move nodes quickly.

Exploring alternatives visually changes how you think. While mind maps can help you recall ideas, they also help generate them. Mapping forces you to think about how the domain is organized, often leading to surprising insights. You'll discover things missed at first and others that might be over-represented.

Which is to say: when drawing a mind map, you're visualizing and developing a model. It won't be perfect at first, but externalizing it helps.

In studying hundreds of situations where insights had a meaningful impact, Klein uncovered four conditions that can trigger an insight:

- Recognizing connections
- Recognizing coincidences and curiosities
- Recognizing contradictions
- Creative desperation

The last of these can be triggered by imposing deadlines; the other three are modeling skills you can hone. A knowledge garden is an ideal place to practice. You're building a note-taking system composed of granular, interconnected ideas: a perfect medium for fostering connections, curiosities, and contradictions.

Tools for Insight Generation

While insights can come at any moment, they're more likely to appear under some conditions than others. As you've already seen, you think with your body, environments, tools, and other people. Some are better suited for some types of thinking than others.

Sometimes you want to think about big ideas. But at other times, you want to work through their implications or consider how to communicate them. Some tools and methods support some of these activities better than others.

Writing offers a good example: sometimes you're brainstorming whereas at other times you just want to write. We use the word "writing" to describe the process as a whole, but brainstorming and typing words to form sentences manifest different mindsets that are best served by different tools.

Applications like Microsoft Word and Google Docs are designed to allow writers to compose and format text: you can write sentences, bold or italicize words and phrases, copy-and-paste between paragraphs, create bulleted lists, insert pictures, add citations, spot grammatical and spelling errors, etc.

These are important activities, but they only cover part of the process. If you're writing nonfiction, you'll research and synthesize before hitting a word processor. Traditional word processors are *production* tools: they help you put down the words when you know what you're writing about. You can think of them in contrast to *thinking* tools—i.e., tools that help you think about what you're trying to communicate.

Use the Right Tools for Thinking

Eastgate's Tinderbox is an example of a thinking tool. While you could write a draft in Tinderbox with many of the niceties of a word processor, that's not its primary purpose. Instead, Tinderbox helps you think through the ideas you're writing about. It does this by focusing on the structure of the concepts you're working with and how they (might) relate to each other—that is, it's a modeling tool.

When I started working on *Duly Noted*, I only had a high-level vision about what the book would be about and some ideas that supported that vision. I'd scribbled notes in a (paper) notebook but didn't yet know if or how they'd flow. There were many important things I didn't yet know about.

Dumping what I knew into Tinderbox was an important early step in the process. By making ideas more tangible, I could explore relationships and identify patterns and gaps. This allowed me to see what might be missing, which let me design a research plan.

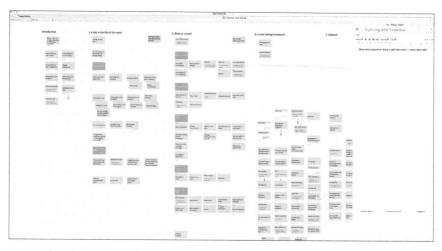

I explored the relationship between ideas in this book using Tinderbox, which acts in some ways like sticky notes on a digital whiteboard. Yellow notes represent ideas and stories, orange notes represent possible section headings, and the vertical gray bars represent possible chapter groupings. Note that at this stage, I'd only really thought through Chapter 2.

Later in the process, I made a second board to explore the book's structure and cadences. Rather than Tinderbox, I made this second board using Apple's Freeform app. While Tinderbox is more capable, I wanted to test Freeform, which had just come out. Also, starting from scratch allowed me to revisit earlier choices and shift my perspective. (More on this later in the chapter.)

The point isn't using these particular apps but having places where you can collect ideas and explore relationships between them. It doesn't need to be an app at all: some people do this with index cards or sticky notes. Externalizing your models helps you think about the work differently than if you barged straight into writing in a word processor.

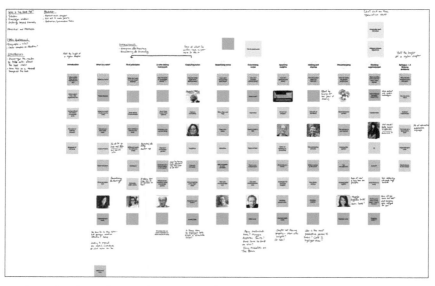

The outline for *Duly Noted*'s second draft, built using Apple's Freeform app. As with the board for the first draft, the vertical columns represent book chapters. Different colors indicate different types of content: conceptual distinctions, exercises, introductory sections, and general notes.

WORKING NOTE

Canvas View

Often, you just want to set ideas down in writing. For example, you may have found a memorable quote in a book and want to remember it later. Conventional (i.e., text-based) note-taking apps such as Apple Notes, Google Keep, and Obsidian are ideal for this use case. But sometimes, you want to capture ideas visually.

For example, the book might lead you to a new understanding of the subject. Rather than capture it in writing, you want to draw a picture that represents the main concepts and how they relate to each other.

You can draw such models using sticky notes on a whiteboard. But there are also digital tools designed specifically for this use case, including Tinderbox, Miro, Mural, FigJam, and Apple's Freeform app. But you don't need to venture far to find a canvas for your thoughts: Obsidian, too, has a mode that enables you to draw models. To use it, make sure that the Canvas core plug-in is enabled. Then click the "Create new canvas" button in the main toolbar.

To use Obsidian's canvas view, click on the "Create new canvas" button in the main toolbar.

CONTINUES ➤

CONTINUED ➤

The canvas interface is similar to what you've seen when composing regular text notes in Obsidian. However, rather than type text into the canvas, you drag objects that can be of three types: cards (which are like sticky notes), references to other notes from your vault, or media assets (such as images) from your vault. You'll see three buttons along the bottom edge of the canvas that allow you to drag any three of these onto the canvas.

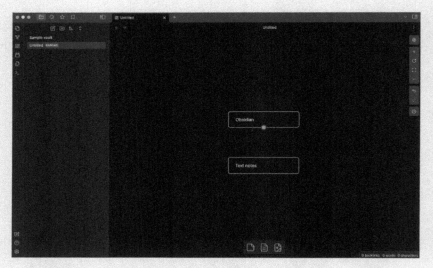

Two cards in Obsidian's canvas view. Note the circular handle at the bottom of the topmost card: this appears when you hover your mouse over the card.

When you hover over cards, you'll see handles appear on one of the card's edges. If you click-and-drag on this handle, you'll see an arrow that can be pointed to another card in the canvas. This is a convenient way of establishing a visual relationship between ideas. If you double-click on one of these arrows, you can add a label to the link. The result is a neat diagram of a conceptual model.

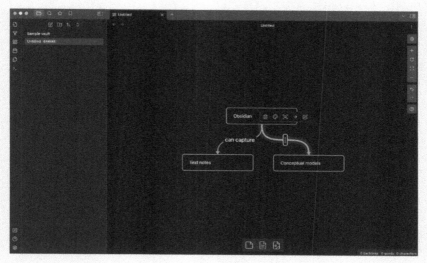

You can add labels by double-clicking on arrows.

Some people brainstorm more easily by drawing mind maps or concept maps. Obsidian's canvas view offers a quick and easy way to use this thinking modality in the same tool where you're also thinking in text.

Tactics for Generating Insights

Getting in the habit of taking connected notes changes your relationship with ideas: you start thinking in terms of models. When any idea can connect to any other idea, you can transcend subject boundaries. Here are a few tactics that will shift how you engage with information, unleashing your creativity and sparking insights.

Read "Outside the Lines"

Many people seek to become experts in a few areas, whether professionally or personally. They "go deep" on the subject, reading everything they find or watching countless hours of YouTube videos. After a while, they learn a lot about the subject.

While developing deep know-how is important, you should also learn about seemingly unrelated fields. If you're into software engineering, consider learning about music or painting. If you learn primarily through reading, get out and visit a museum, a zoo or aquarium, or an unusual shop. Switch things up.

Talk with other people. Collaborating with others exposes you to diverse viewpoints that will break you out of your comfort zone. We'll delve more deeply into collaborative thinking in Chapter 10. For now, suffice it to say that healthy relationships are a powerful means for extending your mind.[3]

Look for Patterns

Connected notes let you focus on individual ideas without thinking about the bigger picture. That is, you can capture ideas without knowing how everything will fit together. Later, you can zoom out to take in the whole. When you do, you can see patterns. For example, you may find one subject coming up repeatedly in different guises.

---

3. Books and lectures are a form of engagement with other people—some of whom might be long dead.

While it's possible to sense such patterns by reviewing your notes, some note-taking apps give you the ability to visualize connections among notes. By making link-node graphs visible, you can identify clusters around topics or types of notes and see how they relate to other types of notes.

For example, in laying out the content for this book visually using Tinderbox and Freeform, I could spot which chapters needed more work than others. I could also rearrange ideas into more obvious sequences.

Uncover Latent Connections

When working on a note, you can link it to other notes, often focusing on connections you can think of at the moment. But there might also be connections to things you've captured in the past but don't remember. Software can help you identify these latent relationships.

For example, I've read lots of material about hypertext in the process of researching this book. I index my notes using DEVONthink, which includes an AI engine that suggests possible relationships between documents based on their contents. In searching through my repository, I found a note about a book I read almost a decade earlier, George P. Landow's *Hypertext*.

DEVONthink's AI suggested a possible relationship between this note and highlights from an interview with Alan Kay in the ACM *Queue* magazine. It included a quote from Kay that influenced my thinking in this chapter:

> All creativity is an extended form of a joke. Most creativity is a transition from one context into another where things are more surprising.[4]

The idea that there's a relationship between contexts and creativity led to a few insights that informed this book. In this case, the computer didn't generate the insight. Instead, it surfaced a latent connection between ideas, some of which I'd captured many years earlier and didn't remember making. This is more than merely outsourcing memory: the computer finds connections among ideas.

---

4. Stuart Feldman, "A Conversation with Alan Kay: Big Talk with the Creator of Smalltalk— and Much More," *Queue* 2, no. 9 (2004): 20–30.

DEVONthink shows a selected document. In this case, it's a note about a book. The right panel shows a list of documents in my database that might somehow be related.

Highlight Curiosities

The flip side of identifying patterns in ideas is the opposite: spotting outliers. Sometimes ideas fit in nicely with the rest of your notes. But some ideas stick out as unusual or unexpected—and spotting them can lead to insights that shift your thinking.

For example, I keep meeting minutes for work-related meetings in Obsidian. I've created note templates that let me quickly fill in details for each meeting, including the list of participants, the project the meeting is related to, and tags that identify whether it's a meeting with my team or with a client.

This format served me well for a couple of years. But recently, I've started being more intentional about reaching out to my friends and colleagues just to catch up. This led me to realize my note-taking system isn't set up for tracking personal relationships.

```
● ● ●                                  untitled text
⚙ (New Document) ⌄                                      ✎ ⌄ ◧ ⌄ ▤
   1   # 2022-10-13 Title
   2
   3   ## Participants
   4
   5   - [[FirstName LastName]]
   6
   7   ## Minutes
   8
   9   This is where I enter the meeting minutes|
  10
  11   ## References
  12
  13   Project: [[ProjectName]]
  14
  15   #meeting/internal #meeting/external
  16
```

A simple template for meeting minutes. Notice that participants' names and the
project name are in double brackets, meaning that they will be turned into links
to other notes. There are two tags at the bottom: one each for internal and external meetings. When capturing meeting minutes, I pick one and delete the other.

My friends aren't a "project" or an area of focus. I don't want to nudge myself
into considering them in the same frame as my professional relationships,
which can be more transactional. This outlier made me reflect on the role
that friendship plays in my life and led me to change how I capture notes
about meetings with friends.

Change Frames

Contexts don't just affect creativity; they also change how you understand
information. To continue with the previous example, you interpret a com-
ment made in a catch-up call with a friend differently than if she said it in a
work meeting. You bring different expectations to interactions at work.

Another way to change contexts is by role-playing. You can ask yourself
questions such as "What would I do if I were a customer?" or "What would a
reader be thinking at this point?" By considering ideas from someone else's
point of view, you can imagine how they play out in different situations,
leading to insights.

Bottom line: when studying an idea, consider the context in which you
found it. You can then envision the idea in a different context to see what
new directions might emerge. Keeping atomic, connected notes allows
you to easily explore the implications of individual ideas in completely
different contexts.

Change Perspectives

A time-tested approach for generating insights is examining ideas from different perspectives. Sometimes this might mean literally moving your body to see things from a different vantage point. But more often, you can shift perspectives metaphorically.

Imagine making an outline for a research paper. You add items in the order that you expect them to come in the paper: first, the introduction, then part one, followed by part two, and so on. Some items might have sub-items, some of which might also have sub-items. Representing these hierarchies is one of the advantages of outlines and mind maps of the sort you saw earlier.

But outlines aren't the only way to visualize this type of information. For example, you could also build a matrix using sticky notes on a whiteboard. While the outline and the matrix contain the same information, they represent relationships differently: the outline shows parent-child relationships, whereas the matrix categorizes ideas along two dimensions.

Shifting your focus between the two modes helps spark insights. Returning to the research paper example, you might visualize the material organized by topics or themes rather than the intended sequence of the paper, leading you to realize you're including more material about some topics than others.

While the idea of shifting between representational modes might sound fanciful, it's one of the main conceits of one of my thinking tools, Tinderbox. Using Tinderbox, you can explore relationships between ideas using outlines, maps, charts, timelines, matrices, and more. You can shift easily between views, and changes you make in one view appear in others in real time.

By shifting perspectives, you can also change your level of focus. You can concentrate on details at one moment and later zoom out to take in the whole. Both vantage points give you different understandings of the material, and moving back and forth between them will help you spot gaps in your reasoning.

Shifting perspectives can be challenging. You likely have stances that feel most comfortable to you. Some people are detail-oriented, while others prefer to dwell in big-picture thinking and may get bored with minutiae. (I'm in the latter camp.) But developing the ability to shift from one to the other enables you to see things differently.

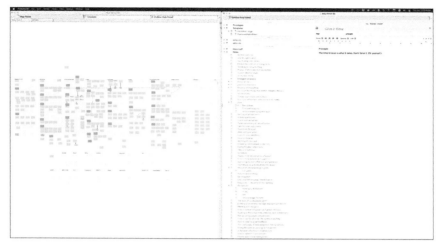

I worked out most of the ideas in this book using Tinderbox. On the left, you see a map view of the key ideas in the book. The right shows an outline of the same data. Changes in one view affect the other.

Embrace Happy Accidents

The word "accident" has negative connotations: it implies things going wrong—sometimes disastrously. You don't plan to have accidents; they happen and can derail you. In this way, they are like insights—but obviously, you want to foster insights and avoid accidents.

While many accidents are, indeed, disastrous, some minor accidents can helpfully shift your thinking. Enter the "happy accident," an idea that creative people of all stripes have embraced for a long time. For example, Alexander Fleming discovered penicillin when he noticed that mold had contaminated a petri dish.

You can intentionally induce happy accidents. In the 1970s, music producer and artist Brian Eno collaborated with the painter Peter Schmidt on a deck of cards called *Oblique Strategies* that features one instruction per card. When a creative person such as a musician, painter, or author is stuck, he or she pulls a card and follows the instruction.[5]

---

5. My favorite Oblique Strategy speaks to the power of the happy accident. The card reads: *Honor thy error as a hidden intention.*

Introducing chance into your work can generate ideas and connections. In writing this book, I've serendipitously come across books, papers, people, YouTube videos, etc. that have expanded my thinking.[6] Some of them provided examples, while others revealed important gaps in my knowledge. These "happy accidents" improved my thinking.

Engage Your Body

We've already covered the role of the body in thinking, but it's worth emphasizing that knowledge isn't just in your head. The rest of your body plays a key role. Becoming more aware—and intentional—about the state of your body will make you more attuned to insights.

If you've been sitting thinking about things for a while, go for a walk. (You may want to take a pocket notebook.) Or take a warm bath or shower. Turn on music and dance around. Take a nap. Engage your senses: run your hands over coarse fabric or light a scented candle. Take off your sweater and feel the temperature change on your skin.

Your body is your primary instrument. Take care of it. Exercise and avoid substances that muddle your thinking. You won't think effectively—much less generate insights— when you're sick, tired, or under the influence of drugs or alcohol.

Keep an Open Mind

You may have noticed a pattern in the strategies I've suggested so far: they require an open mind. While many people pay lip service to the idea of being open-minded, they unwittingly lapse to groupthink. And ironically, knowledge capture systems can make matters worse by formalizing (and hardening) your thinking.

The point of building a knowledge garden is to amplify your mind. But don't confuse amplification with standardization. You want the machine to serve you, not you the machine. Question the systems you're building and remember they exist to serve your humanity—and not the other way around.

---

6. Of course, these encounters were not completely random; I noticed because I was already thinking about this subject and was primed to look for connections.

NOTABLE NOTE-TAKER
Andy Matuschak

Andy Matuschak is a software engineer, designer, and researcher who works on "technologies that expand what people can think and do." He helped build iOS at Apple and led R&D at Khan Academy, and now is an independent researcher developing tools to help people think better. He publishes his working notes at https://notes.andymatuschak.org, an excellent example of a hypertextual note-taking system.

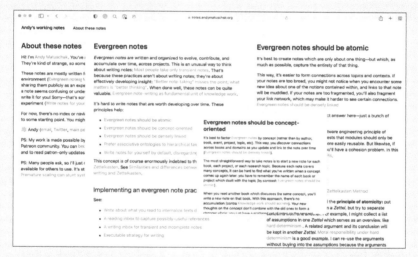

"Andy's working notes" is a public repository of hypertext notes that use an ingenious user interface designed and developed by Matuschak. Hovering over a link reveals a thumbnail preview of the linked note, and clicking on a link opens a panel to the right of the current note. Past notes are stacked on the left. This scheme allows the reader to explore new paths while keeping the original context in sight.

CONTINUES ➤

CONTINUED ➤

Since his work focuses on researching better tools for thinking, these public notes are worth exploring not just for their structure but also for their content. "'Better note-taking,'" he writes, "misses the point; what matters is 'better thinking.'"[7] It's a key reminder: your note-taking system isn't an end in itself. Instead, your notes should serve as a tool that augments your cognitive abilities.

7. https://notes.andymatuschak.org

Endnotes

People mostly think of notes as a way of remembering stuff. But notes can also be a powerful means for generating ideas. Visualizing relationships between them and shifting them around lets you see things from different perspectives, sparking valuable insights.

Mendeleev explored the relationships between elements by moving around cards for each element. He tried different configurations until he could spot the relevant patterns. You, too, can spark insights by organizing and re-organizing ideas, whether in a matrix, a mind map, or a graph. Laying out ideas visually will allow you to spot patterns, identify outliers, and possibly identify missing dimensions to your explorations.

Ultimately, your knowledge garden is more than an extended memory: it's a means for thinking more broadly. Much of it happens while you're reading, studying, or ideating by yourself—which might be good enough. But you may also want to share what you've learned. So far, we've covered how you can use notes to remember and generate ideas. Now, let's turn to sharing those ideas to elicit feedback that will make them stronger.

8

Share Your Thinking

So far, we've discussed thinking as an individual activity. But sharing ideas with other people is essential to thinking. Feedback changes your understanding in useful ways. Many people share small snippets throughout the process. But many also work toward sharing something bigger: a book, a course, a YouTube series, etc. This chapter focuses on sharing your thinking via such larger projects.

In his book *Meditations*, Roman emperor Marcus Aurelius offers advice for understanding stuff:

> always make a sketch or plan of whatever presents
> itself to your mind, so as to see what sort of thing it is
> when stripped down to its essence, as a whole and in its
> separate parts; and tell yourself its proper name, and
> the names of the elements from which it has been put
> together and into which it will finally be resolved.[1]

---

1. Marcus Aurelius, *Meditations: With Selected Correspondence* (Oxford: Oxford University Press, 2011).

Marcus's advice is still relevant: he's suggesting you make models of the sort we described in Chapter 7. But he really isn't talking to you. *Meditations* wasn't meant for publication. Instead, the book consists of notes the emperor wrote to himself, likely as a way to recall worthwhile ideas and perhaps as a mental exercise.

Meditations is a case of private notes made public. Most published work is intended for publication. And conversely, most people likely assume their notes will remain private. People take notes as part of the process of making something meant for publication, but few want their working notes shared.

Sharing what you learn has value in itself, but publishing also improves ideas by exposing them to other minds. Putting your thinking into the world lets you contemplate ideas from different perspectives. People will let you know what you missed or got wrong: a great gift when you're looking to build knowledge.

First Principles for Publication

What you make—and how you do it—depends on your *intent*. For example, suppose you want to write a book. There are several reasons why you might want to do so: perhaps you care deeply about the subject, want to bring leads to your consulting business, or are looking for prestige and wealth.[2]

You'll make different kinds of notes depending on your motives. If your goal is burnishing your brand, you might give a ghost writer a few notes. But if you're writing a Ph.D. dissertation, you'll spend years diving deeply into your subject. Both cases call for different processes, tools, and mindsets.

Publication Requires Iteration

Many people believe that creating work for publication means sitting down to write. Then, after much lonely toil, out pops a manuscript ready for the printers. While that may be true for some people, most writing doesn't happen like that.

Writing is a form of thinking. Often, the work starts with a hunch and perhaps a set of unstructured ideas. Moving from that initial mess to something worth publishing entails iterating over models—sets of interrelated ideas about the subject. Making a model lets you see what you know and what you

---

2. Don't do it for the money.

need to research. As you learn more, you change the model. Each iteration nudges you to develop different parts of the material.

Eventually, you concretize ideas by writing a draft. That first draft is all wrong. Its purpose isn't to be perfect, but to get ideas out of your head where you can see them and iterate some more. Eventually, you get to something that's good enough to share with others. That, too, will undergo iterations as you get feedback. In short, the work entails iterating through different ways of thinking and working. As you do, the work gets closer to something worth publishing.

Understand Your Audience

Earlier in the book, I suggested that you take notes for "future you": a version of yourself that exists in a different context and has different interests. Even though future you is in some ways a different person, it's still *you*. There's a lot of context you can take for granted when writing for yourself.

That's not the case when writing for publication. By definition, you're working to be understood by other people, which requires that you understand their needs and expectations and curate your ideas to meet people where they are in their lives.

Producing a major work like a book entails revealing a curated path through a space of ideas. You can imagine it as a network of related concepts, stories, principles, etc. Your job is to guide the reader through one slice of this space. One person might want to see only anecdotes; another might care about practical skills; yet another might want to be entertained. As author, you decide what to emphasize and when.

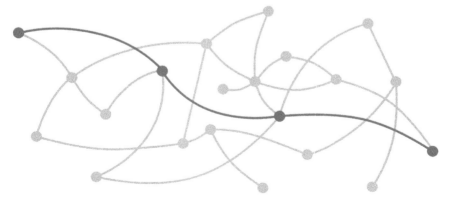

Highlighting one possible path among many in an idea space.

Which is to say, to communicate effectively, you must understand your readers' needs: what they care about, what they know and don't know, why they're engaging with the material, etc. Then you can choose which of many possible configurations works best.

Select Tools That Support Your Intent

As you saw in Chapter 7, some tools help you think about relationships between ideas, while others are better for composing those thoughts for publication. When it comes to publishing, some tools are better suited for developing the style (e.g., layout, typography) of your content than its substance.

The distinction between style and substance feels elusive because many popular content creation tools conflate them. PowerPoint and Keynote are good examples: I've seen people think through what they want to say by typing out slides full of bullet points.[3] When you're sorting out your thoughts, you shouldn't be concerned with how things will look in the end.[4]

Which is to say, producing a major work for publication entails several stages. Each one calls for different tools and practices, and your notes play a different role throughout. In the next section, we'll explore tools and processes you can integrate into your knowledge garden to support each stage in the process.

The Production Process

The process of producing something meant for publication, such as a book, presentation, or YouTube video, follows five steps:

1. Gestating
2. Researching
3. Structuring
4. Drafting
5. Revising

---

3. I've done it, too.
4. This isn't to suggest that good ideas *never* arise late in the process. I've had important insights that shifted my thinking while working on "final" drafts. Again, keep an open mind.

Digital Gardens

I've used the phrase *knowledge garden* throughout this book, but there's another type of note-taking garden you might have heard about: *digital gardens*. Although the concepts are similar, there's an important difference between them: personal knowledge gardens are private (hence "personal"), whereas digital gardens are public.

Digital gardens are somewhat like blogs in that they're personal publications. But while blogs are usually structured as a sequence of essays presented in reverse chronological order (i.e., most recent first) and often grouped in topical categories, digital gardens are hypertexts of the sort I've described in this book—sets of short interconnected notes.

Another important difference is that authors rarely update old blog posts. But notes in digital gardens are meant to evolve as their authors learn more. They are *evergreen notes*, only public. Knowing they'll be seen by other people forces authors to think differently about their ideas. Also, it opens them up to feedback from others at an early stage of development.

"Andy's working notes," which you saw in Chapter 7, is an example of a digital garden that uses bespoke software. Obsidian provides a service called Publish[5] that turns your vault into a public digital garden. There are also third-party plug-ins and scripts that allow you to publish your notes. And other tools, such as Notion and Roam can publish without the need for extra steps.

5. https://obsidian.md/publish

Gestating

Gestation is the beginning of the process: you have an idea about something you want to publish and nurture it from the first spark through to development. At first, the idea may be vague and unformed—and one of many you're exploring. Over time, it might grow into something larger and more structured.

Duly Noted spent several years gestating. My initial hunch was that the work of structuring websites and apps (which is what I do) might yield useful insights for organizing personal information. In researching the subject, I realized that I might be onto something.

Whenever I found something related to this idea, I wrote it down. I stored these notes in a folder I'd made for the book. I have many such folders, each representing potential projects. They're inside a folder called *Incubating*, which I review occasionally. Most of the ideas in this folder won't make it past the gestation stage.

Researching

Some ideas do make it past gestation. Perhaps you find evidence corroborating the idea or get enthusiastic responses when you tell other people about it. Whatever the case, you decide you want to pursue the idea. The next step is researching the subject more deeply.

Long-form works, such as books, require lots of up-front research.[6] What have others written about this subject? How does your experience mirror (or differ) from other people's experience with the subject? What other ideas might substantiate (or negate) the hypothesis? Etc.

Steven Johnson, author of several acclaimed nonfiction books, also reads in preparation for writing. He makes separate notes or ideas he comes across and saves them in DEVONthink, which suggests other possibly related notes. This approach allows him to discover potential relationships between ideas.[7]

---

6. I'm referring specifically to nonfiction books. I don't have experience writing fiction.
7. https://stevenberlinjohnson.com/tool-for-thought-b12c170fcc24

Structuring

Having gathered enough information, you start spotting patterns and gaps. Some ideas might be clustered with other ideas, suggesting possible groupings in the text (i.e., sections, chapters). Others might be outliers that lead to different avenues of exploration to further research.

Notes also play an important part in this stage. But instead of capturing ideas to remember them later, you're looking to externalize ideas to define relationships and distinctions between them. There are two main approaches you can take: outlining and mapping.

You likely learned about outlines in school: you organize ideas in a hierarchical tree. Maps are two-dimensional representations of relationships between ideas, whether using sticky notes on a whiteboard or an application like Freeform. We covered much of this in Chapter 7, so I won't rehash it here.

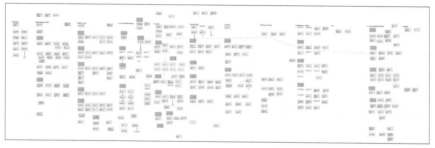

A zoomed-out view of my Tinderbox file for this book later in the project's evolution. Note that at this point I've thought through the organization of several other chapters, although some still look sparse. This high-level view of the entire book is extremely valuable.

Drafting

Drafting occurs when you sit in front of the (metaphorical) typewriter to hammer out sentences. That is, you put ideas into a form others can follow. This stage also entails thinking, and the tools you select change how you think. A key distinction here is between linear and nonlinear tools.

Traditional word processors, like Microsoft Word and Google Docs, assume the thing you're working on is a page of text. This works well for short documents but isn't ideal for long texts, such as books, which often call for revising the overall structure. In tools like Word, moving a block of text from the beginning of a long document to the end entails scrolling a lot. As a result, you're disincentivized from moving stuff around.

An alternative is a nonlinear editor like Scrivener or Ulysses. Rather than focusing on crafting prestructured documents, these apps start from the premise that long documents consist of short texts representing individual ideas, and that the sequencing of those texts can't be defined up front.

While nonlinear editors let you write page-level texts like the linear editors, they also let you work on the document's overall structure, making it easy to move stuff around to experiment with different sequencing. Steven Johnson wrote a memorable description of the difference between working with traditional word processors and tools like Scrivener:

> Conventional word processors don't have a natural way of managing that evolution from hunch to narrative. They lock you into a scrolling document structure from the beginning. They give you a line, not a nest. They give you a medieval scroll when what you need are Chinese boxes.[8]

When you work on a large project, seeing its structure at different levels changes how you think about the material. Nonlinear editors like Scrivener and Ulysses allow you to focus on writing without worrying about where ideas fit into the narrative.

These tools are to MS Word as Obsidian is to a paper notebook: they let you break out of linear thinking to develop individual ideas and connect them in different ways. They also blur the line between structuring and drafting, so you have to be more aware of them when you're working in each modality.

8. https://medium.com/s/workflow/writing-books-isnt-processing-words-f1294120e28f

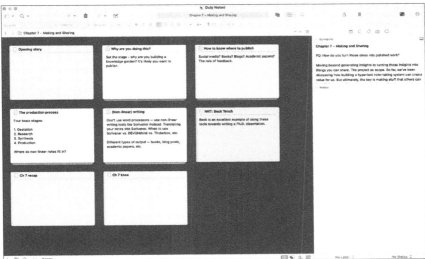

Two views of this chapter's manuscript in Scrivener. The first view focuses on a granular section of the chapter, while the second shows cards that represent the chapter's sections at the highest level. Note that when I captured these screenshots, this was slated to be Chapter 7 in the book. It's not uncommon for authors to experiment with different structural configurations; one of the advantages of nonlinear writing tools like Scrivener is that they make it easy to make such changes even late in the writing process.

Revising

The process doesn't end with a draft. You must then get feedback and make whatever corrections are necessary. You might do this by yourself (e.g., by reviewing what you wrote the day before) or by showing it to another person.[9] If you're lucky to work with a great editor (like I am), you'll get actionable comments that improve the work.

This process doesn't just happen once. As with many other types of work, drafting improves iteratively: you write a draft or sketch a diagram and show it around. You change it based on the things you hear and then show it again. In each round, the work becomes clearer.

This feedback often comes in notes. When sharing a manuscript for someone to review, you'll likely send them a PDF, MS Word file, or copy of the document in Google Docs. All three allow readers to annotate the document with marginal notes. They might include questions about the material, suggestions for improvement, confusing points, etc.

These notes are similar in form to the ones you take when reading a book. But there are important differences. The most obvious one is that you didn't take them, so you must remind reviewers to provide clear notes. Another important difference is that these notes are tied to specific parts of the work, so you must go through them in linear order.

This makes the process tedious, especially if several people provide feedback. Often, you must go through several individual annotated copies of the work. I hope that AI will someday ease the process of giving and receiving feedback. But for now, consider that this part of the process will take longer than you expect.

Don't shortchange it. Even though feedback comes toward the end of the process, it's essential to ensure that the work communicates what is intended. Also, as you'll see in the next section, it's an essential means for learning. If part of your reason for building a knowledge garden is to keep learning, you must build in feedback mechanisms.

---

9. AI can also help here. But as of this writing, the technology is new enough that I can't write firsthand about getting feedback from AI.

Publish a Book Review

In Chapter 2, I suggested you start a note to capture your thoughts as you read this book. These reading notes are valuable per se. But since you're likely reading by yourself, your notes only include your thoughts. What if you could also benefit from the things other people have learned?

One way to expand your understanding is by sharing your thoughts with other people. By publishing your ideas, you can engage in discussion, exposing you to different takes on the material. Some will broaden or deepen your understanding; others will cause you to reevaluate your positions. Either case benefits your thinking.

Writing notes for publication is different than writing them for yourself. For one thing, writing for yourself doesn't require as much explanation, since you've now got context about the book. When sharing publicly, you can't assume the reader has read the book, so you must explain the basics:

- What is the book about?
- What is the author trying to do?
- Were they successful? Why/why not?

Answering these questions forces you to consider the book's premise. Did you get it well enough to explain it to others?

After establishing baselines about the book's subject, you can share your thoughts. What did you learn? Did the ideas in the book spark connections with other things you know? Get them down. Add references to other works. If you've published several such book notes, you can cross-reference them, slowly building a network of ideas. Because they're public, you will eventually attract people drawn to similar books.

CONTINUES ➤

CONTINUED ➤

There are lots of ways to publish. You can start a blog to share long-form thoughts or use a microblogging service, such as Twitter or Mastodon, for shorter takes. You can also review them in bookseller sites like Amazon. People interested in the book are more likely to look for it there than in your blog, so you're more likely to find thoughtful takes on the subject in Amazon. (Of course, you're also likely to see reviews that aren't as useful.)

If you're engaging with *Duly Noted*—positively or negatively—consider writing a review in Amazon. Don't just post something that says, "I liked it"—tell us *why* you liked it. (Or not.) Revisit your private notes. What has stood out? How have these ideas changed you? Why does that matter?

Peruse other reviews. Do any already cover what you were planning to say? If so, consider what might be a fresh perspective. As you do, revisit your private note about the book to add what you've learned from reading others' reviews. The Amazon book page is part of a global feedback loop about this book—one in which you can participate.

The Role of Feedback

Even though we've emphasized the distinction between tools for thinking and production tools, thinking happens throughout the process. Making and thinking aren't separate activities. In fact, you think by making. Putting ideas into the world, and seeing how the world responds, changes how you see them.

Think back to a time you made a presentation deck, one slide at a time. Seeing the sequence of ideas in the deck may have led you to realize some things were missing. Or you may have shown the slides to a colleague, who suggested taking some stuff out. Both are examples of feedback.

What's the Point of Feedback?

If you're like many people, the word "feedback" probably brings up negative feelings. It may remind you of that time your manager asked, "Can I give you feedback?" followed by what seemed like unpleasant criticism. Or, if you're into music, feedback might remind you of the ear-piercing sound of a microphone placed too close to a loudspeaker.

Neither of these are pleasant associations. But feedback is an important concept from systems thinking that will make your work better. The gist is cause-and-effect: you do something and then get information about the results of your action so you can react appropriately.

Envision dribbling a basketball. At first, you hold the ball in your hands, feeling its texture and tautness. You feel the hardness of the ground beneath your feet. Your eyes see the ball as you throw it. When it hits the ground, it makes a distinctive sound. Its quality also informs your expectations about the ball's possible trajectory. This is all information about the situation.

All this happens in less than one second. You don't think about it. Instead, your body knows what to do based on what you perceive and your previous experience with basketballs. You act (i.e., throwing the ball), and the world reacts with visual and aural cues that help you predict how the ball will move.

These sounds, sights, and tactile feelings are feedback. By paying attention, you can act more skillfully: you adjust your body to receive the ball, throw the next bounce slightly faster or slower, and so on.[10] If you repeat the process many times, you'll become better at handling the ball—all thanks to feedback.

How to Overcome the Feedback Dilemma

It's one thing to learn to dribble a basketball—a relatively low-stakes activity—and another to publish your ideas. Giving a public presentation or publishing a book can make you feel vulnerable. We identify with our ideas, which is why the word "feedback" can bring up negative emotions: it can feel like being criticized.

So, here's a dilemma: your work won't get good without feedback, but you may be apprehensive about sharing before your work is good. You have to get the cycle going somehow. One way around this dilemma is to become comfortable with sharing half-baked ideas, which requires reframing the production process.

The traditional way of undertaking a big production is to go "heads down" for a while, isolating yourself until you have something worth sharing. Then,

10. This is why "keep your eye on the ball" is common coaching advice.

when the artifact is "good enough," you share it with other people for feed-back. This requires that you get a lot of things right from the start, since you can't correct course until you've put in a lot of time.

An alternative is to share ideas as you go, allowing feedback to influence the work throughout the process. For example, if you're writing a book, you can set up a blog to share specific ideas while you work on them. Readers don't expect blog posts to be as fully thought-through or documented as books, so they'll give you more leeway. And if your blog supports it, they can also leave comments.

While writing *Duly Noted*, I shared many ideas on social media and my news-letter. The people who responded gave me a sense of which topics resonated and which fell flat. In some cases, folks also pointed me to ideas or books I'd missed at first. I learned a lot about this book's subjects by sharing my half-baked ideas early.

Where Should You Look for Feedback?

Of course, sharing ideas early doesn't mean you must publish them for the whole world to see. You can limit the audience for ideas until they've been stress-tested by trusted collaborators.

In his *Personal Knowledge Mastery* framework, Harold Jarche advocates shar-ing ideas as a way to grow knowledge.[11] He distinguishes between three levels of sharing, ranging from most intimate to most public:

- **Work teams,** who develop joint knowledge toward shared goals
- **Communities of practice,** consisting of trusted individuals who share the same context
- **Social networks,** which expose more refined ideas to other perspectives

There's a natural progression here: you stress-test fledgling ideas with peo-ple you trust so you can develop them before sharing more widely. You start with close collaborators before moving to groups who share your context and then finally to the world at large. Each step helps you correct misunder-standings, reinforcing ideas and increasing your confidence.

---

11. https://jarche.com/2014/02/the-seek-sense-share-framework/

Maggie Appleton

Maggie Appleton is a UX designer, developer, and anthropologist. She also publishes insightful and accessible illustrated essays about subjects like artificial intelligence, transclusion, and digital gardening.

The latter brought Maggie's work to my attention. Not only is her essay on digital gardening a great introduction to the subject, but Maggie is also a practitioner: her personal website[12] includes a section called *The Garden*, "A collection of essays, notes, and half-baked explorations I'm always tending to."

That is, *The Garden* features public notes about ideas in various stages of development. You can filter ideas by topic, type (e.g., notes, essays, patterns), and growth stages (e.g., evergreen, budding, seedling). The site is in active development; when I last checked in, the latest idea had been "planted one day ago."

Patterns, essays, and notes in *The Garden* have different structures. Notes and essays are freeform, with the latter being longer. Patterns, on the other hand, have more structure: they have sections devoted to describing the pattern's relevant context in addition to the pattern's main content. Some also have links to examples and descriptions of the intended audience.

CONTINUES ➤

12. https://maggieappleton.com/garden

The main page of Maggie Appleton's *The Garden* shows its navigation and filtering features.

One of the challenges of browsing public digital gardens is that they can be hard to navigate and parse. Personal notes-to-self often take for granted lots of context, so they don't make as much sense to other people. Digital gardens' emergent structures can make information hard to find. But Maggie clearly gave a lot of thought to making *The Garden* accessible to new readers. The site blurs the line between public note-taking space and polished publication.

Endnotes

When writing notes in my knowledge garden, I sometimes think of Richard Harris, who played Marcus Aurelius in the film *Gladiator*, scribbling thoughts into a notebook by a flickering candle. Marcus lived in a different world and used comparatively primitive technology. But like you and me, he used things to extend his mind. You can "read his mind" because his notes have been made public.

Most notes aren't. I took a lot of private notes in preparing for this book. Those notes aren't the point; the point is thinking leading toward the book you're reading now, which synthesizes ideas collected and nurtured over many years. My role has been to steward them, curating and sequencing them to (hopefully!) communicate clearly with you.

Knowing there are distinct stages to the production process—and which tools and methods best support each stage—was essential to working effectively with these ideas. And, of course, sharing them isn't the end of the process: I hope to get feedback from you and other readers that broadens and deepens my thinking.

You may wonder what I'll do with this feedback. After all, the book is done. Obviously, I'll feed it back into my knowledge garden. My understanding will continue to evolve for as long as I live. Along the way, I'll come across new ideas and technologies to support them. Which is to say, the garden itself needs to continually evolve. The next chapter explains how to set up your garden so that it changes and grows to support your evolving needs.

9

Tend the Garden

O ver time, your knowledge garden becomes richer and more complex. You learn new things, your needs change, technologies advance. The trick is evolving the system without wasting time fiddling with tools. The goal isn't better gardening but better thinking. This requires discipline.

In his classic children's book, *The Little Prince*, Antoine de Saint-Exupéry tells of an encounter between the narrator, an aviator stranded in the Sahara, and a child who has mysteriously emerged from the desert. The aviator eventually realizes the child—the titular little prince—is a visitor from another planet. It's a small planet, but it keeps him busy:

> "It's a question of discipline," the little prince told me later on. "When you're finished washing and dressing each morning, you must tend your planet. You must be sure you pull up the baobabs regularly, as soon as you can tell them apart from the rosebushes, which they closely resemble when they're very young. It's very tedious work, but very easy."

Why baobabs? The prince goes on to explain:

> "Sometimes there's no harm in postponing your work until later. But with baobabs, it's always a catastrophe. I knew one planet that was inhabited by a lazy man. He had neglected three bushes…"[1]

Left unattended, routine chores become large problems: baobabs overtake planets, weeds smother flowers, teeth rot, the electricity gets cut, etc. And so it is with your knowledge garden: you must continually work at it. This happens on two levels:

- Day-to-day maintenance of system structures and content
- Periodic upgrades and replacement of system components

Both rely on clear principles and habits. We'll get into those. But first, a word of warning: there's a difference between *work*—the stuff you're trying to do—and *meta-work*—all the stuff that supports that work.

Meta-work Enables All Stages of the Process

One of the pitfalls of knowledge gardening is that it's easy to spend more time working *on* the system than working *in* the system. By working on the system, I mean things like tweaking settings, evaluating new tools and processes, reorganizing your tags, etc. These are important activities, but they're no substitute for the actual work of thinking.

Complex systems need maintenance and organization. When you work, things quickly get disorganized. To illustrate with an analogy: cooking a big meal messes up your kitchen; preparing your next meal will be easier if you tidy up after you're done.

Like the kitchen, your knowledge garden is a place set aside for a particular purpose: thinking better. The process can get messy, and you must occasionally tidy up: inboxes must be cleared, books returned to shelves, index cards filed, etc. Then you'll be ready—physically and mentally—for the next project.

Recall the diagram introduced in Chapter 4; each stage in the process requires some degree of maintenance.

---

1. Antoine de Saint-Exupéry, *The Little Prince*, trans. R. Howard (New York: Houghton Mifflin Harcourt, 2000).

Notice

Pay attention to ideas and observations that come to mind as you go about your life.

Capture

Take down thoughts and observations you may have to revisit later.

Sort

Go through your note app inboxes to get notes to the right places — or toss them if no longer needed.

Retain

Keep ideas worth revisiting in the appropriate trusted repository.

Nurture

Revisit notes to identify and establish connections between related ideas.

Share

Make something that adds to the world's knowledge and share it with others for feedback.

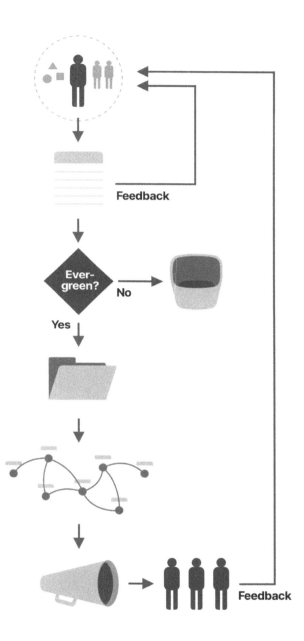

Feedback

Ever-green?

No

Yes

Feedback

For example, if you capture things using a (paper-based) pocket notebook, you must occasionally review those notes for ideas and actions that need to be moved into your knowledge store and to-do lists, respectively. And when you run out of empty pages, you must buy a new notebook and store the old one where you can find it, if needed.

The sorting stage requires particular attention. As mentioned previously, inboxes only serve their purpose if they're *temporary* holding places. The point isn't to store things there permanently, but to hold them until you're ready to do something with them.

For example, I like to take some kinds of notes using pen and paper. One such case is when I interview someone for my podcast. Afterward, I scan these notes using my phone, which syncs them to a folder on my computer where they're automatically imported into my DEVONthink.

Around once a week, I go through this inbox and tag and file everything in it. Sometimes I might skip a week if I'm too busy, but if I wait too long, stuff will pile in there. Clearing the inbox will be more burdensome, which leads me to put it off until later. A vicious cycle ensues.

How do you determine the right cadence for each process? A key factor is whether somebody else might be waiting for a follow-up. I'm the only person impacted by the stuff in my DEVONthink inbox. However, people might be waiting for replies to things in my email inbox, so I process that more frequently. Another factor is how quickly things come into your inboxes. If you're adding only a couple of notes per day, you can get away with sorting the inbox weekly. But if you're capturing dozens of notes every day, weekly may be too long to wait.[2]

It helps to give yourself reasons to clear your inboxes. For example, I send a newsletter every other Sunday that includes links to articles and tools. I regularly capture these links in DEVONthink and tag and archive them when preparing the newsletter. The project gives me a recurring deadline for clearing this inbox.

2. This doesn't imply you should act on everything in your inboxes on the spot. Some things require immediate follow-up, but others can wait. Don't use inboxes to track to-dos or commitments. For an excellent book on how to effectively manage your commitments to self and others, I recommend D. Allen, *Getting Things Done: The Art of Stress-Free Productivity* (New York: Penguin, 2015).

Common Tasks That Demand Meta-work

So, you want to go through your inboxes fairly frequently. However, that's not the only task that requires meta-work. If you're aware of things that need maintenance, you'll be better able to balance your time between focusing on your work and focusing on the system that enables the work to happen.

Manage Containers for Focus

As you may recall, you keep inboxes clear by moving items to more permanent containers such as folders, directories, and groups. They keep your notes out of your way for now while still making it possible for you to find them in the future.

Left untended, containers, too, will accrete. If you create a new folder whenever you start a project, over time, you'll have lots of folders. This makes clearing your inboxes harder, because more folders increase your cognitive load when deciding where things should go.

But the fact that a project has ended doesn't mean you should get rid of its notes or files. You may want to refer to the information in that folder in the future, so you should still keep it around.

The solution is to keep dedicated containers for things (e.g., projects) that are no longer active. For example, I have a *Projects* folder on my Mac. The first folder in the *Projects* folder is special: it's called *_Archived*.[3] That's where all the inactive projects go. Every time I finish a project, I move its folder from the *Projects* folder to the *_Archived* sub-folder. It's a little ritual that gives me satisfaction: my commitments are done, and I'm ready to make space for other things. I know where to find it later if needed, but it isn't commanding my attention day-to-day.

---

3. Note the underscore character before the word; this allows me to keep this container at the top of views that sort folders alphabetically.

Keep Container Names Consistent for Findability

As you saw in Chapter 6, it's important to name containers consistently so future you can find them more easily. Because I'm a consultant, my project folder naming pattern looks like this:

Client name - Project name

I keep both parts of the name as short as possible while still being distinctive. For example, if I'm redesigning a website for a company called *Acme*, I'll create containers called *Acme - Web redesign 2022*.[4] I wrote *containers* in plural because I'll reuse this name in various places: folders on my Mac and my to-do tracker, cloud services such as Google Drive, etc.

Keeping container names consistent across apps is another routine maintenance chore that will keep your system organized. It's not the sort of thing you do on a predictable schedule, but rather when called for. Be disciplined about it: if you change the name of the folder later, change it everywhere else you're using it.

Stay on Top of Sync

Many people use more than one device for note-taking. If you're on the run, you'll likely capture thoughts on your phone. But when you're working on projects, you'll likely use a device with a bigger screen. It's important to ensure that your information is syncing properly between devices.

This isn't as much of an issue if you're using cloud-based SaaS ("software as a service") products, such as Notion or Roam Research, since your information will be in remote servers anyway. But if you're using file-based apps, such as Obsidian or DEVONthink, you want to ensure that all instances of the app have the latest versions of your notes.

Review your containers and inboxes once in a while to make sure they have the latest versions of your stuff. Few things are as annoying as realizing you're working with old data because your devices stopped updating data days (or weeks!) ago. If you're not using cloud-based apps, check in on your app's sync status every once in a while.

---

4. You may wonder about the year at the end. I sometimes do this because I aim to have long-term relationships with clients. In some cases, I've helped them with similar projects over several years. Again, the idea is to make these names minimal yet distinctive; in this case, I'd want to easily distinguish the 2022 project from one we worked on in another year.

Scan Your Paper Notes

If you're like most people, you sometimes take notes on paper. They present an additional hurdle: before they go into your digital knowledge garden, you must either transcribe or digitize them. This can be a chore, and it's one of those things that gets worse the longer you wait.

I've tried many means of inputting physical notes into my computer. The big breakthrough was phone scanning apps. Phones have excellent cameras that make fast work of scanning. Coupled with smart software, the process becomes easy. As a bonus, you can do it anywhere.

The best app I've found for phone-based scanning is Readdle's Scanner Pro.[5] (Caveat: there's a similarly named app for Android from a different company. I can't vouch for it, but there might be apps in that ecosystem that provide similar functionality.) I like this app because it makes the process fast and easy.

With a desktop scanner, pages lie flat against the device's scanning surface. As a result, the digitized image is captured head-on. You don't have that luxury when scanning on your phone. Instead, you take the picture while holding the device above the document, often at an angle. Scanner Pro corrects for this by finding the document's edges and tweaking the picture's perspective to make its edges parallel.

The software activates this feature automatically and snaps the picture when you're steady and have a clear shot. So, you just hold the phone until it takes the picture, flip the page, and do it again. The process is faster than using a flatbed or duplex scanner. You can save in a variety of formats, such as PDF and JPG and apply filters to scanned documents (for example, to make them black-and-white for highest contrast).

5. https://readdle.com/scannerpro

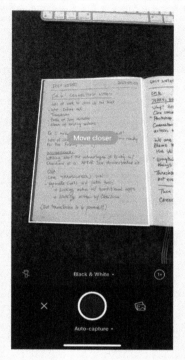

Scanning a page from my notebook in Scanner Pro. The app has detected the page's edges and suggests I get closer so it can get a clean shot. When the image is clear enough, it will snap the picture and correct the perspective. The process takes seconds and can be done anywhere.

But Scanner Pro's most valuable feature might be automatic OCR (optical character recognition). OCR detects typographic characters in the image and saves them as text. Usefully, this also works for handwritten notes. (At least it's great for me—I expect this feature depends on the clarity of your handwriting.)

Evolving the System

So far, we've covered routine maintenance chores. But every once in a while, you'll also want to change the system's components. Your needs change over time, and new technologies provide different capabilities. The key is to change things without breaking your flow.

To return to our kitchen analogy, sometimes you want to replace an appliance. Perhaps you've read about a fancy new toaster oven that accommodates larger pizzas. Or maybe your freezer isn't working properly. Or—in extreme circumstances—you decide to redo the entire kitchen. Some of these changes are more disruptive than others. You may buy a new coffee grinder on a lark. But replacing your in-wall oven is a major project that will likely require research, cost lots of money, and entail expert help. You want to make such major changes infrequently and only for good reasons.

Revisiting our process diagram, the "big components" are where you retain information for the long run—where your ideas "live" permanently. You don't want to change these too frequently. In particular, you don't want to do anything that breaks links to individual notes and documents.

In my case, I keep knowledge stores in two applications: DEVONthink and Obsidian. I picked this pair in part because of how well they interoperate (more on that shortly). But it's worth acknowledging that one of these apps (DEVONthink) is only available on devices that run Apple operating systems.

In fact, some important apps in my knowledge management system are only available on one of Apple's operating systems: macOS. As a result, the most disruptive change I could make to my setup would be switching to a different operating system.

It's important to understand which parts of your system are unchangeable. I won't change my OS, since it would mean too much trouble for little upside gain. But this might not be a constraint for you if you use cloud-based apps such as Roam Research or Notion.

Obsidian stores notes as plain Markdown files in a user-accessible folder. DEVONthink understands Markdown and can index files in any user-accessible folder. As a result, you can see and manipulate Obsidian notes in DEVONthink.

How do you know if it might be time to replace a system component? Here are three reasons for moving on:

- **The app is being discontinued, or its maker is going out of business.** This is obviously a bad situation; you're facing disruption for little gain. It's preferable to avoid this situation altogether. One way to do so is to choose apps from larger, more established companies.[6]

- **Your needs have changed.** Perhaps you've started teaching part-time at a university or have decided to write a book. In either case, your current apps might lack features you need, such as tracking bibliographic references.

- **Exciting new features are available elsewhere.** Sometimes, a new app will come along that promises to do magical things. Perhaps it's an AI breakthrough that could make archiving automatic or a new search engine that lets you find things faster. Whatever the case, you want "the new shiny."

---

6. One of my two main knowledge store apps, Obsidian, is made by a small team that doesn't yet have a long track record. But it has a vibrant community and—more importantly—stores data in an open format, making it very portable in case I need to migrate.

These reasons are listed in order of most to least pressing. You can't rely on an app that's being discontinued and should look to replace it soon.

Evolving needs are also a good reason to change, although you might consider whether your current apps truly can't meet your new requirements. (It might be useful to search the web for suggestions on how to do what you're trying to do using your existing app.)

The third reason should give you pause. Do you really need this snazzy new feature? Will it really do for you what you expect it to do? Remember: you won't get much benefit from knowledge gardens until you've added lots of notes. This takes time.

Also, consider that many innovative new apps are made by young companies that don't yet have a track record or, in some cases, even a viable business model—which brings you right back to the first point in the list.

You should be more conservative with some aspects of your knowledge management system than others. Replacing a major component will cost time and money. You'll have to learn new ways of doing things. Eventually, you might be more efficient than you were before the change—but it will take time to get there.

In other words, such changes are meta-work, not work. And as always, you want to strike a healthy balance between the two. Fiddling around with new tools may be fun, but that's not why you're reading this book.

Principles for Selecting System Components

So, you've decided it's time to change one of your system's components. How do you choose one app over another? These nine principles will help:

- Avoid lock-in.
- Favor interoperability.
- Look for automation/scriptability.
- Favor trustworthy providers.
- Look for vibrant communities.
- Work with the technology's grain.

- Avoid "everything" apps.
- Avoid process disruptions.
- Start small and look for tools that "satisfice."

Avoid Lock-in

Look for tools that allow you to take your data with you should you decide to move. This entails letting you export your stuff in standard formats that can be read by other apps. You should also prefer tools that enable you to back up your data.

Favor Interoperability

Look for documented APIs and standards-based import/export capabilities. As noted previously, Markdown has emerged as the preferred markup language for connected note-taking. At a minimum, system components should be able to read and write Markdown-formatted text.

Look for Automation/Scriptability

Some tools give you the ability to automate routine tasks. While you may not use such features when starting out, they can save you lots of time when you've become more proficient. Look for tools that expose features and functionality to your operating system's automation capabilities.

Favor Trustworthy Providers

You're looking to build a system that serves your needs in the long term. This implies looking for providers that have a trustworthy trajectory— i.e., they've been around for a while, have business models that respect your attention and privacy, etc.

Look for Vibrant Communities

Some tool providers are relatively new, so they don't have a long track record; however, they've managed to build vibrant user communities. Look for tools that allow users to contribute plug-ins and extensions and have passionate users sharing tips, YouTube videos, etc.

Work with the Technology's Grain

Some tools are better suited for some needs than others. For example, digital "whiteboarding" tools, such as Mural and Miro, are best used for collaborative visual thinking. Conversely, they're not well-suited to long-form text editing. Don't try to force tools to do things for which they're not well-suited.

Avoid "Everything" Apps

Avoid tools that promise to manage everything for you. If you pick interoperable software, then you can have smaller tools that are best-of-class for particular use cases. Rather than force any one tool to try to do it all, it's better to use several good dedicated tools—as long as they interoperate effectively.

Avoid Process Disruptions

Don't just think about features and capabilities; also consider how the new tool will fit into your processes. For example, if the tool has its own inbox, you'll have to make time to clear it periodically in addition to all the other inboxes you already review. This could add friction to your processes.

Start Small and Look for Tools That "Satisfice"

Economist Herbert Simon coined the useful neologism "satisficing" as a portmanteau of satisfactory and sufficing.[7] Some things are good enough; it's not worth extra time and money to look for more. If you abide by the previous principles, you'll be able to replace system components when you outgrow them.

For now, make do with tools that meet your current needs. Start small and simple and build from there. Your knowledge garden should suffice for your near-term needs and become richer and more complex as you use it over time.

Fiddling around with system components might be fun, but that's not ultimately why you're building a knowledge garden. Whenever you're contemplating changing a system component, ask yourself: "Why do I need this?" Time you spend tweaking the system is time you could use to learn something using the system.

---

7. H. A. Simon, "Rational Choice and the Structure of the Environment," *Psychological Review*, 63, no. 2 (1956): 129–138.

Managing Tags

Earlier in the chapter, we discussed staying on top of folder names. But containers aren't the only elements in your system that need regular maintenance. You should also occasionally revisit your tags.

I say "should" because, frankly, I maintain tags less frequently than containers. For one thing, keeping a few rogue tags in the system is less disruptive than misnaming containers. For another, maintaining tags takes more work than tweaking containers.

As always, you should avoid unnecessary busy work. That said, it's important to occasionally review your tags to ensure consistency.

The main challenge is that apps make it easy to create new tags on-the-fly but editing them later isn't as easy. Apps that support tags usually provide auto-complete functionality, which brings some consistency. But you can also easily keep typing to inadvertently add variations of the word.

An example would be accidentally adding the plural form of a term. Imagine you tag some notes #book. However, later you mistype one as #books instead. The app treats #book and #books as different, so you've added a new term to your taxonomy. When looking at your #book notes, the plural is excluded.

Resolving mistaggings entails reviewing tag lists and correcting errors. When selecting an app to manage notes, look for features to let you tweak tags as a list (i.e., technically, a "controlled vocabulary"). The opposite case—changing tags in individual notes or files—is very time-consuming.

CONTINUES ➤

CONTINUED ➤

The Obsidian ecosystem features a third-party plug-in called *Tag Wrangler* that lets you manage your tags.[8] You can rename tags across all notes, create new pages for tags, hide tags, and more. It's an easy way to make mass changes to tags in your vault. (That said, you must use it with care, since these changes can't be undone.)

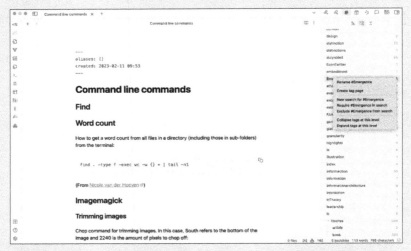

The Tag Wrangler plug-in creates a tag list in Obsidian's right sidebar. From there, you can explore and modify tags in your vault.

8. https://github.com/pjeby/tag-wrangler

Building Sustainable Habits

By now, it may be clear that managing a knowledge garden takes time and effort. Some tasks can be fun, such as experimenting with new components. But others are chores. New technology will help you automate some, but others you'll have to do for a while. The best way to do them unobtrusively is by turning them into habits.

A *habit* is a regular practice you do without thinking about it. Returning to the kitchen analogy: in my home, we use an old school freezer without an ice maker. Whenever we take out the ice, we must refill the ice trays. At first, it was a chore. But we've gotten good at doing it almost automatically.

In *Atomic Habits*, James Clear argues that effective habit formation starts small: you tackle an easy habit first, and when that becomes automatic, you scaffold more difficult or complex habits onto it. Clear explains that lasting behavior entails considering what you're doing on three levels:

1. **Outcomes:** What you want to get out of the behavior change. For example, you might build a knowledge garden because you want to write a book.

2. **Processes:** The day-to-day activities that allow you to "work" the system. For example, capturing your thoughts when they occur to you or clearing your inboxes.

3. **Identity:** How you see yourself anew in light of the behavior change. For example, you now think of yourself as an *author*.[9]

While most of us focus on outcome-based changes, identity-based changes are more powerful and enduring. As Clear puts it,

> The ultimate form of intrinsic motivation is when a habit becomes part of your identity. It's one thing to say I'm the type of person who wants this. It's something very different to say I'm the type of person who is this.

---

9. James Clear, *Atomic Habits: An Easy & Proven Way to Build Good Habits & Break Bad Ones* (New York: Penguin, 2018).

Which is to say, habits stick better when you switch from thinking of things you have to do and think instead of who you want to be. It's one thing to want to write a book and another to become an author. They're related, but you'll be more compelled to change when your identity is on the line.

Here are some principles that will help you implement the habits you need to build a sustainable knowledge garden.

Build One Habit at a Time

Don't change too many things at once. Instead, work on one habit at a time. Later, when you can do it without thinking, you can add another. For example, focus first on clearing your inboxes. When you can do that automatically, you can then focus on adding tags before moving items out of the inbox.

Work with Others

Rather than going it alone, work on your habits alongside a friend or colleague. Publicly committing to a new way of being is a great way to leverage the power of identity. It can also be fun to share your progress with others. (This is why book clubs can help you read more.)

Pick the Right Time and Place

Contexts help establish successful habits. If clearing your inboxes is a chore, why not associate it with a pleasurable place or activity? For example, rather than clearing your inboxes when you're busy, go to a coffee shop on a calm morning and sit for an hour with a warm beverage. Put on some music and get to it.

Do It Now

Some things you can put off until later, such as clearing your inboxes. But others you must do now. For example, you should capture ideas as soon as they occur to you. This requires developing two habits: always having something to write with and paying attention to your ideas. Again, these are separate habits; build them one at a time.

Favor Consistency over Intensity

You'll get greater returns from doing small things repeatedly over a long time than expending great effort in one go. When starting out with a new system, many people spend a lot of time migrating content and organizing things up front. Then they let the system sit dormant for a while as they catch up on all the other things they put off.

It's better to move things over in small increments. For example, try using the new system only for one project while continuing to manage the others as you were. Then, when you're comfortable with the tool, you can move more work onto it.

Delegate Unimportant Stuff

Some things aren't worth your time. Consider delegating or automating as much as possible so you can focus on the things that really matter, such as learning and thinking. An app that's helped me with organizational chores is Hazel, which automatically re-names and moves files in macOS based on conditions you specify. (Other operating systems might have similar apps.)

Work with Your Grain

Earlier in the chapter, I suggested you work with the technology's grain. You have a grain, too. By that, I mean that some things will come naturally to you and others will cause resistance. Developing habits entails changing your behaviors. But that doesn't mean you must force yourself to do things you don't like. Learn to read and pace yourself.

Play the Long Game

Building a knowledge garden is a long game. Results won't come overnight— and won't happen at all if you expect immediate results. As with (physical) gardening, you'll eventually see fruits, but it will take patience and persistence.

NOTABLE NOTE-TAKER

Beck Tench

Your information management needs change over time as you take on different projects and roles. One example is when working toward an academic degree.

When Beck Tench was a Ph.D. candidate, she focused on protecting and restoring human attention. In a series of short YouTube videos, she shared the process of researching and thinking about her dissertation. As Beck put it,

> The actual discovery part—and even more than that, remembering what you've discovered and recalling it at the times when you need to recall it or connecting ideas across discoveries—is really a big deal, a very big part of the work.[10]

She used several tools to keep track of her research:

- The Goodnotes app on an iPad for reading and annotating PDFs
- The Paperpile reference management software
- A paper notebook for capturing insights while reading
- Tinderbox for spotting relationships between insights
- Google Docs for writing

It's not unusual to have different tools for capturing and managing information. Some lend themselves more to capturing information, some are better suited to thinking and connecting ideas, and some are tailored for producing finished texts.

10. www.youtube.com/watch?v=IOWLOMGFAEw

Those needs will change as you move from one step of the process to the next. You'll also learn new techniques as you become more profi-cient, leading to the formation of new habits. Thanks to generous people like Beck, YouTube can be a great source for examples of how to manage your information.

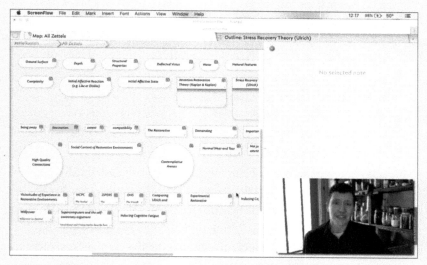

Several of Beck Tench's videos explain in-depth how she used Tinderbox to implement a zettelkasten-like system to manage research insights. They're worth your attention if you're trying to make sense of large sets of insights in preparation for writing a book or—as in her case—a Ph.D. dissertation.

Endnotes

The Little Prince includes a spectacular painting of the prince's planet overtaken by three enormous baobabs. The author explains that the prince himself commissioned the drawing for the edification of children:

> So, following the little prince's instructions, I have drawn
> that planet. I don't much like assuming the tone of a moral-
> ist. But the danger of baobabs is so little recognized, and the
> risks run by anyone who might get lost on an asteroid are so
> considerable, that for once I am making an exception to my
> habitual reserve. I say, "Children, watch out for baobabs!"
> It's to warn my friends of a danger of which they, like myself,
> have long been unaware that I worked so hard on this draw-
> ing. The lesson I'm teaching is worth the trouble. You may
> be asking, "Why are there no other drawings in this book as
> big as the drawing of the baobabs?" There's a simple answer:
> I tried but I couldn't manage it. When I drew the baobabs, I
> was inspired by a sense of urgency.

You must get on top of things before they get on top of you. Just like a physical garden is overgrown with weeds if left unattended, your knowl-edge garden will become a mess if you don't spend time on meta-work. This includes renaming and archiving files and containers, managing tags, clearing inboxes, and doing lots of other menial chores. None are as much fun as learning and making stuff, but they must be done if you're to learn and make effectively.

Conversely, some meta-work poses the opposite risk: it can be fun but creates little value. This includes fiddling with new software, which is always a temptation for people looking to optimize their processes.

In either case, the key is doing things intentionally. Knowing why you're doing something helps you determine whether it's worth your time. Automate as much as you can, whether by using software or by turning chores into habits you can undertake without much cognitive load.

An effective garden is one that grows and evolves as your needs and interests change. In the final chapter, I'll turn toward important future directions your system might evolve into, which includes collaborat-ing with other minds—human and otherwise.

10

Think with Other Minds

Maintaining a knowledge garden needn't be a solo activity. For a long time, people have augmented their cognitive abilities by working with others. Collaboration opens you up to feedback from diverse perspectives that strengthen and broaden your thinking.

For centuries, scholars hired people to assist them. Dutch philosopher and theologian Erasmus of Rotterdam (1466–1536) offers a good example. At first, when he didn't have much money, Erasmus had young boys help as a sort of proto-interns. Later, he could afford to hire helpers to perform clerical duties.

A few of these assistants he promoted to the role of *amanuenses*. They were like super secretaries, performing tasks like taking dictation, copying texts, cleaning up drafts, transcribing messy handwriting, indexing, and managing books. It was a sensitive role that went beyond simple duties.[1]

IMAGE VIA WIKIMEDIA. HTTPS://COMMONS.WIKIMEDIA.ORG/ WIKI/FILE:COGNATUS-ERASMUS.TIFF

Erasmus working with Gilbert Cousin, one of his amanuenses.

We live in a less stratified time, and technology has reduced the need for clerical assistants. As a result, we collaborate with others on a more even level. Also, other people's thinking is more easily available via books, websites, YouTube, etc. And even though most thinking partners throughout history have been human, AI has recently joined the fray. This chapter shows you how to build spaces that support shared generative knowledge work— whether you're working alongside other people or artificial minds.

1. For an excellent treatment of knowledge work in the early modern era, see A.M. Blair, *Too Much to Know: Managing Scholarly Information Before the Modern Age* (New Haven: Yale University Press, 2010).

How Collaboration Changes Note-Taking

Many distinctions I've discussed so far also apply to collaborative note-taking. But working with others requires more up-front planning so everyone can contribute without stepping on each other's toes or getting lost. How you do it depends on what you're trying to do.

Collaborative Capture

Let's start with capturing what you hear or see. The most obvious use case here is where two or more people take shared notes in a meeting, lecture, or interview. The key distinction is that they are *shared* notes: that is, all parties work on the same note simultaneously (as opposed to separate notes that are merged afterward).

The easiest way to do this is by taking notes in real time using collaborative apps like Google Docs or Notion. One advantage of this approach is that it lets you capture more of what was being said. You can see what others type in real time. After a while, you meld like a jazz band. The resulting notes are often more comprehensive and useful than those taken by individuals working alone.

Collaborative Ideation

Collaborative ideation includes brainstorming sessions and workshops. Physical venues for such work often include whiteboards or empty walls for capturing ideas, either by drawing, pasting sticky notes, pinning up sketches, etc.

You've seen how some authors use sticky notes to hash out book structures. The same can be done in groups. Everyone is "on the same page," surrounded by the ideas that emerged from the session. Participants can point to ideas, move them around, group them, explore gaps, explore alternatives, etc.

Cloud-based "infinite canvas" applications like Miro, Mural, and FigJam make remote collaborative ideation feasible. Unlike physical rooms, software boards can be kept up after the workshop is over, making long-term ideation feasible, and they also provide almost infinite space.

Collaborative Gardening

Brainstorming sessions are a means for joint sense-making and alignment. But they tend to be one-offs, often meant to move a project forward. But there are also collaborative knowledge gardens: shared environments for nurturing ideas over the long term. Some are public, but most are kept within the walls (er, networks) of organizations.

For example, *Scaling Synthesis* is a "living hypertext notebook" authored by Rob Haisfield, Joel Chan, and Brendan Langen. Their goal is "to find data structures and interfaces that support synthesis and innovation in a decentralized discourse graph"—that is, they are using a shared public hypertext to think about how to think collaboratively using shared hypertexts.[2]

Experiments like these are rare. Synthesizing ideas collaboratively requires lots of shared context, real-time updates.[3] It's more likely you've experienced such systems in apps like Notion or SharePoint, which organizations use to document projects, HR policies, IT processes, and more. Users can share and edit information in ways that look more like knowledge gardens than top-down publications like websites.

How to Organize Shared Thinking Spaces

When you're working alone, you can organize things in whatever order makes sense to you. But when you're collaborating, you should think about how other people will find and use stuff. Just as it's hard to get anything done in an unfamiliar, messy room, it's also hard to collaborate in a messy thinking space. This is where information architecture (IA) can help.

Information architecture is a design discipline focused on organizing and labeling information to make it easier to find, use, and understand.[4] It requires understanding how people think about particular types of information. For example, orthopedic surgeons categorize information about the

2. https://scalingsynthesis.com
3. https://scalingsynthesis.com/c-synthesis-is-hard-to-do-with-people-who-dont-share-context-with-you/
4. Louis Rosenfeld, Peter Morville, and Jorge Arango, *Information Architecture for the Web and Beyond* (Sebastopol: O'Reilly Media, 2015).

Keep Thinking Spaces Organized

Where thinking happens, the setup of the space itself influences *how* thinking happens. When you're thinking by yourself, you can get away (and perhaps even thrive) with a messy workspace. But the more people you bring into the process, the more the space's structure matters. An organized space makes collaborative thinking easier.

While this applies to physical spaces, it also applies to Miro boards or Google Docs. People might meet simultaneously or drop in once in a while to leave comments and notes, move stuff around, draw lines connecting ideas to one another, etc. As a result, it's easy to lose contextual clues.

As a result, you must be more intentional about organizing and maintaining digital collaboration spaces. You should alternate periods of thinking work with housekeeping. Designate someone to be the space's maintainer. Walk new collaborators through the space's structure and encourage them to keep it organized.

body differently than dancers. Designing systems usable by either audience requires understanding of their needs and expectations.

While I don't expect you'll do heavy IA work while organizing shared thinking environments, at a minimum, you should consider your collaborators' perspectives. How do they expect stuff to be grouped? What should categories be called? How often will those things change?

For example, I often use digital boards to share the progress of design projects. They include sections devoted to project stages such as research, modeling, and ideating. Within these, I set aside areas for different kinds of artifacts (user personas, content audits, web page sketches, etc.). Each area has large labels to make them easy to identify even when zoomed out. I encourage participants to add new content from left to right, so the most recent work is easy to locate.

These boards evolve over time as needs change. For example, a project might need more space for sketches. But as long as you stick to clearly labeled structures and a few organizational principles, the board will accommodate changes without becoming a mess. (Obviously, this calls for proactive maintenance of the sort we discussed in Chapter 9.)

AI Assistants

So far, I've discussed collaboration assuming that you're collaborating with other people. But technical advances have made that assumption obsolete. It is now possible to augment your thinking using artificial intelligences. Today's AI systems aren't minds like ours, but that doesn't mean they're not useful.

Before diving into how AI can augment your thinking, I'll state up front that this part of the book won't age well. By the time you read this, some (if not all) of the technologies showcased in the next sections will likely seem primitive. So, rather than recommend specific tools, I'll focus on principles and approaches that are more likely to stand the test of time.

You may have noticed that I referred to "intelligences" in plural. AI is a broad term that encompasses different technologies that help people do knowledge work. Some have been around for decades, but the excitement around recent breakthroughs is centered on new types of systems called *generative AIs* that accept textual prompts in the form of common sentences and produce "creative" output—often successfully.

The successful cases are uncanny in their ability to mimic human abilities. As of this writing, there are lots of open questions about creative ownership, authorial responsibility, social impact, and more, but it's clear these systems— imperfect as they are—can help you think better. The question is, how?

One way to go about it is to consider the role of these systems on a continuum ranging from "no impact whatsoever" to "total replacement."

NO IMPACT ◄――――――――――――――► **REPLACEMENT**

The "no impact" side is the world pre-AI: nothing changes. Obviously, this position is moot now. The other extreme ("total replacement") is not yet feasible—or, in my opinion, desirable. After all, the point of building a knowledge garden is thinking better, not having someone (something?) else think for you. So, you're looking at a point between these two.

There are several positions worth exploring. I've identified three, which I'll map to three roles previously played by humans:

- AI as editor
- AI as ghostwriter
- AI as amanuensis

Let's examine them in more detail.

AI as Editor

Using AI as an editor means having AI check your work, which might include looking for spelling and grammar errors.

For example, many people use grammar and spelling tools to review their work. A more advanced system could alert you to gaps in reasoning or logical fallacies. Such a tool would offer suggestions and let you decide what to do about them. Using it over time would hone your reasoning.

To wit, using Grammarly improved my writing by helping me recognize recurring flaws in my work—a more relevant and compelling context than learning grammar rules in theory. I expect a reasoning checker ("Thinkerly"?) would do the same to my ability to argue cogently. The ethics are trickier than a grammar checker, but not by much.

AI as Ghostwriter

In this position, the AI creates the finished work for you based on short prompts.

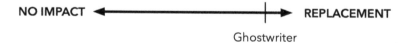

Systems like ChatGPT can write a sonnet on a particular topic or compose essays on the merits of some position. It's uncanny—and a bit terrifying, given the social harms inherent in mass-produced propaganda. There are many ethical concerns with this position, so I don't use AI tools in this capacity.

AI as Amanuensis

This position is the one that excites me the most. I think of it as being somewhere in the middle.

NO IMPACT ←————————————→ REPLACEMENT

Amanuensis

As you saw at the beginning of the chapter, past scholars hired amanuenses attuned to their thinking and needs. AI can be used as digital amanuenses: instantly available research assistants and sounding boards. You can give them questions and sometimes snippets of writing and ask for summaries or suggestions for further reading. Their responses can help clarify your thinking.

For example, I asked ChatGPT to summarize an early draft of this section. Here's what it responded:

> The author of this essay is cautiously excited about AI and ChatGPT in particular. They discuss the ethical implications of using AI to assist with text-based assignments and propose three ways in which AI can be used in the writing process: as an editor, ghostwriter, or amanuensis. The author believes that while complete replacement of human writing is not yet feasible or desirable, AI can be a valuable tool in the writing process.

This interaction validated the clarity of my writing. While I'm not planning to pass AI-generated texts as my own (i.e., the ghostwriter position), I can augment my thinking by interacting with digital assistants that can suggest different avenues for exploration, research materials, and even words and ideas I may have missed. (For example, the phrase "sounding boards" above was suggested by ChatGPT.)

AIs can also help you identify latent connections between ideas and keep the place organized. They can analyze your notes and suggest connections to other notes, possible containers, and answer questions based on your previous notes.

Even though my meaty fingers typed these words, the thinking behind them is a hybrid concoction. Which I think is OK—and perhaps even necessary, given our current state of information overload. But who knows? One way or another, we're blurring authorship and augmentation in weird and interesting ways.

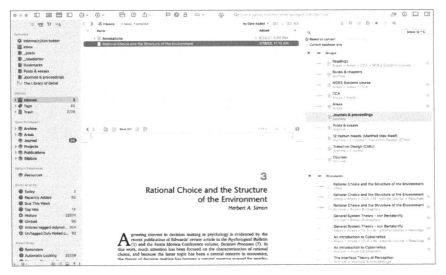

DEVONthink features an AI engine that suggests containers within your database where a document might be stored based on its content.

It's OK Not to Take the Robots at Their Word

A common objection to using generative AI for thinking augmentation is that they sometimes "lie"—i.e., produce assertions that sound authoritative but are wrong. It's a real risk caused by how these things work: they don't think like you and me. Instead, they string together words based on statistical relationships in large data sets.

Using these systems effectively entails understanding what they are—and aren't—well-suited to do. I'm most interested in using them as creative partners. Sometimes, my thinking is clear, and the work is straightforward: I have a well-formed idea and start typing. But often, I have a vague notion and need a better model or examples.

In these cases, talking with someone often helps. I'll bring up half-baked ideas, and the other person will suggest angles I hadn't considered. "Have you thought about this?" they'll ask. Or they'll say something like, "That reminds me of a story…"

These conversations often yield valuable nuggets. The other person isn't thinking for me; they're contributing pieces to a puzzle. Putting the pieces together is my job. While AIs can't (yet?) assemble the puzzle, they can suggest pieces.

AI for Reading Notes

For many years, I've kept a reading log. Whenever I finish a book, I write a note about it with high-level thoughts about the work. Later—sometimes years later—I revisit these notes to recall what I read. At first, they were short: a line or two at most. Over the years, they've become more elaborate. Recently, I've started using generative AIs to help. Here's how I do it.

When I finish a book, I start a note with the book's title, author, publisher, and year of publication. Then I write a summary followed by my observations. For nonfiction, I write the summary myself. But for novels, I now let AI do it. The robot's summary reminds me of the work's plot and themes, making it easier for me to recall outstanding ideas.

For example, I recently read *War and Peace*. It's a long book; at my leisurely pace, it took several months. By the end, I was overwhelmed by details and characters. I started the note with the usual template. Then I asked the AI for a summary. This is what it produced:

> War and Peace [*sic*] is a novel by Leo Tolstoy, first published in 1869. It chronicles the lives of five aristocratic families—the Rostovs, Bolkonskys, Bezukhovs, Kuragins, and Drubetskoys—during the French invasion of Russia. The novel explores themes of Russian culture and society, politics, family life, religion, and the meaning of history. It also features a large cast of characters in various relationships to one another and presents a detailed portrait of 19th-century Russian society at the time of Napoleon's invasion.

This text went into the beginning of my note, preceded with a tag that indicates that what follows was written by a robot. This keeps me from inadvertently passing it off as my own in the future.[5]

---

5. There's a possibility the AI itself may be passing off somebody else's text as its own. This is yet another reason to clearly separate AI-written text from your own.

This snippet helped me recall the book's themes: "Russian culture and society, politics, family life, religion, and the meaning of history." That last theme reminded me of a thought I had while reading the book: that major historical developments are highly contingent; history assigns more agency to figures like Napoleon than they merit. So, I captured that idea in the note as well.

This is a good use for AI. For one thing, I'm not asking the system to read for me; there would be little point in that. For another, this use case is less susceptible to hallucinations; I'd know if the system invented stuff since I know what the book is about. And even if the AI spouted nonsense, I'd catch it. (I've already read the book!) Correcting the robot's mistakes forces me to check the original or other sources, which is valuable per se.

So far, this approach has worked well, but I've only started recently. Also, this approach likely works best for well-known works like *War and Peace*. The quality of the AI's summary depends on its training corpus, and there's more written about classics than more obscure works.

Even though you could use ChatGPT to do this, there's a third-party Obsidian plug-in called *Text Generator* that lets you call GPT language models directly inside your notes. With the plug-in installed, you type a line of text in a note (e.g., "The novel War and Peace by Leo Tolstoy is about") and then press a button. After a few seconds, GPT's summary appears in the note. (Similar features exist for other note-taking apps, such as Notion.)

Again, the point isn't having the AI read for me; there's no fun in that. And obviously, the summary doesn't do justice to the entire work. But that doesn't mean there's no value here. It's great to start with more than a blinking cursor on a blank screen. Not a draft but a memory nudge—an augmentation, not a replacement.

Currently, my primary use for AIs is as conversational partners. My prompts aren't along the lines of "Write an essay for me about x in the style of y," but rather "What's a good example of x?" The system then suggests ideas or stories I hadn't considered.

This works well, with the caveat that sometimes the ideas or stories may be factually wrong. (People sometimes are wrong, too!) But it's OK since I'm not planning to pass off the AIs' output as fact; I'm only using them to prime my creativity.

Writing is thinking. And although I don't expect to use systems like ChatGPT to write for me, composing finished texts isn't all that writing entails. Developing ideas is an essential part of the process, and generative AIs can serve in this role as intellectual—if sometimes unreliable—partners. The fact I can bounce ideas off them clarifies my thinking and sometimes points me in new directions. This is valuable per se.

Everything Is a Remix

As you saw earlier, much thinking work is collaborative—even if it doesn't seem so on the surface. As you read these words, you and I are collaborating in a way: I'm offering you ideas, some of which you'll make your own. Most aren't my ideas: I, too, have collaborated with others to bring them to your attention. I've met some of these people, but most are long dead; our collaboration happened via their published work.

Which is to say, truly new ideas are rare. Your models are comprised of ideas developed by others, who in turn developed them from others. You internalize these ideas and make them your own by adding nuances or different takes. By sharing these ideas, you invite other people into the conversation.[6]

Who Owns the Output?

One of the controversial aspects of generative AIs is that they're trained on other people's ideas, casting doubt on the ownership of their "original"

---

6. After writing this section, I was made aware of the *Everything Is a Remix* video series, which focuses on recombining previous works as a creative endeavor. For more, see www.everythingisaremix.info

output. In some ways, this is how your brain, too, works; AIs just do it at a much larger scale.

In many cases, you'll use other people's ideas unwittingly. I don't know where I first heard the word "unwittingly," but, of course, I didn't invent it. If I had to cite each word's provenance, we wouldn't be able to collaborate; our conversation would quickly devolve into bottomless (and pointless) discussions about attribution.

That said, credibility and fairness require that you cite provenance. For example, throughout this book, I've included footnotes and citations referencing other books and resources where I found the stuff I'm discussing. These references convey a latent message: I didn't make up the models I'm sharing; they're a patchwork of ideas developed by other people. My job is to synthesize and clarify them to help you do something.

Track Your Sources

Citing provenance comes down to noting where you found things. This is one reason for capturing atomic notes: your knowledge garden can include one note for a book or paper and lots of other notes for ideas you found in that resource. By linking ideas to their sources, you can track down their provenance. Later, when writing an essay, blog post, book, or video, you can reference the original sources.

This is an idea I picked up from Niklas Luhmann, via Sönke Ahrens's book *How to Take Smart Notes*:

> Strictly speaking, Luhmann had two slip-boxes: a bibliographical one, which contained the references and brief notes on the content of the literature, and the main one in which he collected and generated his ideas, mainly in response to what he read… Whenever he read something, he would write the bibliographic information on one side of a card and make brief notes about the content on the other side (Schmidt 2013, 170). These notes would end up in the bibliographic slip-box.[7]

Ahrens differentiates between "literature notes"—notes taken while reading—and "fleeting notes" and "permanent notes," both of which we

---

7. Sönke Ahrens, *How to Take Smart Notes* (Createspace Independent Publishing Platform, 2017).

discussed in Chapter 2.[8] Literature notes are an important means for capturing what you've learned from a particular source. Ahrens explains them thus:

> Whenever you read something, make notes about the content. Write down what you don't want to forget or think you might use in your own thinking or writing. Keep it very short, be extremely selective, and use your own words. Be extra selective with quotes—don't copy them to skip the step of really understanding what they mean. Keep these notes together with the bibliographic details in one place—your reference system.

Whenever I read a book or paper that influences my thinking, I start a new note where I capture general thoughts about it. But I also start separate notes for specific ideas I get from the book and link them to the book's note. I use different templates for these notes: I call the former *literature notes* and the latter *evergreen notes*. Each template includes tags (#litnotes and #evergreen) that identify them as such.

For example, I have a note for *How to Take Smart Notes* that includes data about the book itself, its author, when it was published, a link to its Amazon page, and its identifier in Bookends, software I use to manage references. This note also includes my overall thoughts on the book. But I also have several evergreen notes that capture ideas I learned about in this book. These notes link back to the book's general note.

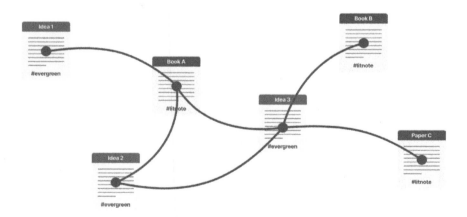

8. I prefer the term "evergreen" for permanent notes to keep the organic metaphor in play.

The result is a rich network of ideas and references. When I circle back to use or develop an idea later, I can cite its sources. And, of course, I can add links to other relevant papers or books to a note, revealing connections between ideas and works. The garden becomes a venue for ideas to meet and cross-pollinate, often yielding valuable fruit.

NOTABLE NOTE-TAKER

Jeremias Drexel

Portrait of Jeremias Drexel S.J. (1660), via Wikimedia Commons

With the printing press, books and pamphlets became inexpensive and widespread, giving independent scholars easier access to information. With more information to process, they had to come up with better means to manage ideas. One such scholar was the preacher and writer Jeremias Drexel (1581–1638), whose writings on note-taking remained influential until the early 19th Century.

Drexel was an avid reader and note-taker, boasting of taking notes from 100 or even 600 authors in a day. He believed note-taking aided memory in two ways: first, because writing out a passage helps you retain it, and second, because the notes themselves serve as a record you can return to later.

CONTINUES ➤

CONTINUED ➤

Ann M. Blair, scholar of early modern information management techniques, describes Drexel's approach thus:

> [He] recommended maintaining at least three quarto-sized notebooks—one for bibliographical references, another for passages of rhetorical interest, and a third for historical exempla—each provided with an alphabetical index in a separate, smaller notebook. Drexel also suggested drawing up two indexes per notebook in order to separate the profane from the sacred topics and keeping separate notebooks for different fields, including medicine, law, mathematics, philosophy, or theology.[9]

Proliferating notes meant the scholar could keep track of what they'd already written. Thus, indexes became an invaluable memory aid. Dealing with newly abundant information called for new methods and techniques. As Blair put it,

> One of the achievements of early modern pedagogues and scholars was to experiment for the first time in considerable numbers with the bulk storage of notes and with the methods of sorting and retrieving them that made them usable.[10]

Which is to say, we aren't the first people dealing with exploding information access. Drexel and his contemporaries learned not just to cope with the stuff but thrive in it. I suspect he would've recognized—and applauded—the drive to build knowledge gardens using hypertextual note-taking software.

9. Blair (2010)
10. Idem

Endnotes

Although it may appear lonely, knowledge work is a collaborative enterprise. Thinking alongside other minds doesn't only happen in real time; you get lots of ideas from books and other media—a form of time-delayed collaboration.

At one point, Erasmus had a staff of eight people assisting with knowledge work. Many people can't afford that expense. But technology has obviated the need for many of the most mechanical aspects of knowledge work. And AI promises to help with many higher-level tasks as well.

Current AI can't yet take on tasks that require judgment, but technology is constantly improving. Perhaps by the time you read these words, digital amanuenses will help you think in ways my contemporaries and I can barely imagine.

As you build your knowledge garden, look for opportunities to learn from and collaborate with others. And conversely, consider sharing what you learn. You are part of the world's rich intellectual diversity. The ultimate knowledge garden spans the whole world—and you can seed it today.

Epilogue

A book is a learning journey. This is obviously true for the reader, but it's also true for the author. I've worked *with* and *on* the ideas and practices in *Duly Noted* for years. Sharing them with you has forced me to organize and synthesize my thinking.

One key takeaway is that what I initially saw as a convoluted set of technologies and practices boils down to three simple rules:

1. Make short notes.
2. Connect your notes.
3. Nurture your notes.

In these rules, "notes" is a proxy for ideas. You're not building a note-taking system, but rather a way to capture, explore, and generate ideas.

Thinking clearly is essential to living a good life. It's hard to do when immersed in environments designed to claim your attention. Building a personal knowledge garden is an invitation to take control of the information in your life so that you can use it more skillfully.

Your needs will change over time. You'll encounter new ideas and people. New technologies will bring amazing new capabilities to the mix. With some discipline and a spirit of exploration and play, your garden will evolve into a thinking space that brings it all together and nourishes you for the rest of your life.

You have what you need to get started. Now go and make something wonderful.

Index

gardens. *See also* knowledge garden

   collaborative knowledge, 166

   digital, 127, 137–138

Gardner, Jessica, ix

Geertz, Clifford, 31

generation of ideas, as note-taking
   purpose, 3

generative AIs, 168. *See also* AI (artificial
   intelligences) assistants

*Genius: The Life and Science of
   Richard Feynman* (Gleick), 14

gestation, in publication
   production process, 128

Getting Things Done (Allen), 56, 83, 145

ghostwriting by AI, 169

Gladiator (film), 139

Gleick, James, 14

Goodnotes, 160

Google Docs, 108, 130, 160, 167

Google Keep, 111

GPT language models, 169, 170, 172–173

Grammarly, 169

Greene, Robert, 6

H

H/LAMT, viii

habits, formation of, 157–159, 161

Haisfield, Rob, 166

happy accidents, in generating
   insights, 119–120

Harris, Richard, 139

Hazel, 159

highlighting, in annotating books, 7, 70

The History of Navigation (Locke), 85

van der Hoeven, Nicole, 81–82

Holiday, Ryan, 6, 7

How to Take Smart Notes
   (Ahrens), 61, 175–176

HTML, 25–26, 42

hyperlinks, defined, 38

"Hypertext Gardens" (Bernstein), xiii

Hypertext (Landow), 115–116

hypertext note-taking, xii, 34–35,
   46–47. *See also* connecting notes

hypertexts

   links and nodes, 38–39, 41–45

   living hypertext notebook,
     Scaling Synthesis, 166

   origin of term, 35

I

ideas, as notes, 181. *See also*
   capturing ideas

implicit links (link type), 41–42

inboxes

   clearing out, 95, 144–145

   in media for capturing notes, 73

   piling notes in, 87–88

   for sorting notes, 56, 59–60

index cards

   as media for note-taking, 6

   paper-based systems using
     linked nodes, 39

   slip box (zettelkasten)
     system, 61–62, 65, 175

indexes

   beginnings of, 178

   finding information, 87

"infinite canvas" apps, 107, 165, 167

Acknowledgments

This book wouldn't exist in its present form without the contributions of my friend and colleague Karl Fast. Karl has been a wellspring of inspiration before, during, and after the writing process. Any ideas here that seem especially lucid likely emerged from our conversations. Thank you, Karl!

Along with Karl, Andy Polaine and Nicole van der Hoeven provided deep reviews of early drafts. As experienced connected note-takers, their comments proved practical, inspiring, and reassuring—at a time when all were needed. The following people also provided feedback and encouragement: Giancarlo Andreani, David Bill, David Daly, Noah Fang, Dave Gray, José Gutiérrez, Tara Kimura, Grace Lau, Liz Massey, David Price, Dawn Russell, Daniel Vieira Souza, Maxime Stinnett, Riccardo Tommasini, Shivanand Reddy Yerva, and Adam Zeiner.

Two decades ago, Howard Rheingold's book *Tools for Thought* inspired me to approach computers as a mind extension technology. Meeting Howard was one of the gifts *Duly Noted* has given me; his generous and insightful foreword is this author's dream come true. Thank you, Howard!

I've had the privilege of interviewing over a hundred experts on my podcast, *The Informed Life*. Their insights on "how to organize information to get things done" have influenced my thinking. I'm especially grateful to those featured or cited in these pages: Sönke Ahrens, Gretchen Anderson, Maggie Appleton, Mark Bernstein, Kourosh Dini, Sam Ladner, Jerry Michalski, Annie Murphy Paul, Beck Tench, and Nicole van der Hoeven. I'm also grateful to Andy Matuschak—whom I haven't interviewed—for his inspirational work and for reviewing the short section about him in Chapter 7.

Marta Justak isn't just the best editor an author could wish for—after two books together, she's also a good friend. Thank you, Marta! Lou Rosenfeld and the Rosenfeld Media team are pillars of stability and professionalism at the fast-changing intersection of design and publishing. This book is an outlier; I'm grateful they've allowed me to test their portfolio's bounds.

Jimena, Julia, Ada, and Elias: thank you for giving me space to cultivate this garden. Every minute I spent here subtracted from our time together—a very high cost.

Duly Noted has my name on the cover, but like all books, it's a remix of other people's ideas. I'm thankful to all of them. I've strived to attribute and represent them correctly—and likely failed at some point. If so, I beg your—and their—forgiveness. Like all knowledge gardens, mine is still a work in progress.

 **Rosenfeld®**

Dear Reader,

Thanks very much for purchasing this book. There's a story behind it and every product we create at Rosenfeld Media.

Since the early 1990s, I've been a User Experience consultant, conference presenter, workshop instructor, and author. (I'm probably best-known for having cowritten *Information Architecture for the Web and Beyond*.) In each of these roles, I've been frustrated by the missed opportunities to apply UX principles and practices.

I started Rosenfeld Media in 2005 with the goal of publishing books whose design and development showed that a publisher could practice what it preached. Since then, we've expanded into producing industry-leading conferences and workshops. In all cases, UX has helped us create better, more successful products—just as you would expect. From employing user research to drive the design of our books and conference programs, to working closely with our conference speakers on their talks, to caring deeply about customer service, we practice what we preach every day.

Please visit ﬀrosenfeldmedia.com to learn more about our **conferences**, **workshops**, **free communities**, and **other great resources** that we've made for you. And send your ideas, suggestions, and concerns my way: louis@rosenfeldmedia.com

I'd love to hear from you, and I hope you enjoy the book!

Lou Rosenfeld

Lou Rosenfeld,
Publisher

RECENT TITLES FROM ROSENFELD MEDIA

Get a great discount on a Rosenfeld Media book:
visit rfld.me/deal to learn more.

SELECTED TITLES FROM ROSENFELD MEDIA

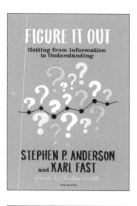

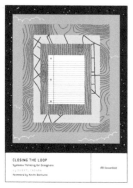

View our full catalog at rosenfeldmedia.com/books

About the Author

JORGE ARANGO is an information architect, author, and educator. For almost three decades, he has architected digital experiences and made the complex clear for organizations ranging from nonprofits to Fortune 500 corporations. He is the author of *Living in Information: Responsible Design for Digital Places* and co-authored *Information Architecture for the Web and Beyond*. In addition to his design consulting practice, Jorge hosts *The Informed Life* podcast, writes a blog, and teaches at the California College of the Arts. You can learn more about Jorge at https://jarango.com.